THE HARROW RAILWAY DISASTER 1952

L. F. E. COOMBS

David & Charles
Newton Abbot London North Pomfret (Vt)

To UNA and her patience

British Library Cataloguing in Publication Data

Coombs, L.F.E.
  The Harrow railway disaster 1952.
  1. Railroads—England—London—Accidents
  2. Harrow (London, England)—History
  I. Title
  363.1'22'0942186   HE1783.G7

  ISBN 0-7153-7409-5

Second impression 1978
Third impression 1984

Printed in Great Britain
by Redwood Burn Ltd
Trowbridge Wilts
for David & Charles (Publishers) Limited
Brunel House Newton Abbot Devon

Published in the United States of America
by David & Charles Inc
North Pomfret Vermont 05053 USA

Contents

Introduction

The Harrow railway disaster happened in 1952, in living memory still of many who today are going about their daily business, to work, to shop or school. It involved three trains and caused the deaths of 112 passengers and trainmen, including some who were waiting on the station platforms or crossing the footbridge; it was a double collision which produced a great mound of wreckage, completely blocking all but two of the seven tracks which passed through this busy North-West London main-line and suburban station and it took the rescuers over two days before they were sure that all who could be rescued alive had been reached. The resulting press and public demands for better safety on the railways were echoed in newspapers, and much ill-informed comment on technical matters was added to the pages printed on the subject of this, the second greatest disaster in British railway history.

Few, if any, human activities are completely free from risk. Death and injury are recognised and even accepted as an inevitable part of life, and insurance companies are the tangible proof that no one thinks she or he is immune from either natural or man-made hazards. In the Middle Ages, in those parts of the world not subjected to great natural disasters, such as flood fire and tempest, or battles between opposing forces, the greatest danger to be faced was that of disease or succumbing to injury or ailment often today regarded as trivial. With the growth of technology man added to the hazards of his life. One activity above all, apart from pestilence and war, which placed a large number of people at risk in conditions far removed from their beds, was transport. Away from home, hearth, field, shop or cloister, men and women increased their exposure to natural and man-made dangers whenever they journeyed. Seas were explored, ships became larger and on occasions a chain of adverse circumstances led to a disastrous collision with an un-yielding rock. On land few were gathered together in one vehicle until the railway became the common form of land transport, and great numbers of travellers were exposed at the same time to mechanical risks, equivalent in their consequences to those previously met only at sea. In retrospect it is easy to be critical of human and mechanical failings because, in general, we tend to learn from past mistakes. Our present world is so different from that even of twenty-five years ago, and things of an earlier time by inference, often seem wrong or inadequate. Criticism is not difficult. The harder task is that of constructive criticism which is one of the objects of this book.

The Official Report into the double collision at Harrow & Wealdstone by the Ministry of Transport has a footnote after Lt-Col G. R. S. Wilson's signature which reads: 'Apart from the 112 persons who lost their lives at Harrow, only one passenger was killed in an accident to a train in 1952.' The cynic reading that might conclude that the gods had decided to exact their penalty from hurrying mankind in one lump.

The public has always expected rail travel to be one of the safest forms of transport. Statistics have proved them right. It is this very fact of the public's expectation of safety by rail which makes any train accident of particular interest and concern. If there were as many accidents on railways as on the roads the public would have long tired of banner head-lines and pages of pictures of wrecked trains. Railways, an important element of the country's economy and life, are not expected to fail in their job of conveying safely every year millions of passengers for millions of miles.

This double collision occurred against the background of a nationalised railway established only four years, in a society and economy just struggling free from post-war restrictions and shortages, and, most significantly, at a time when the final decisions had just been reached on a standard safety system— the automatic warning system (AWS)—for all lines in Britain, intended to reduce the chances of this type of accident happening again. As many writers have pointed out since 1952, this accident and AWS will always be associated in the history of safety on Britain's railways. Although AWS had been developed long before the double collision at Harrow, this tragedy removed the last financial barriers to its extensive installation.

When invited to write this book by Geoffrey Kichenside, of the publishers, who remembers at first hand the great mound of wreckage, I was particularly pleased because of my long interest in the design and operation of railways and, above all, my special interest in the relationship between man and the many different machines he controls. Of all the different control positions among the transport systems of the world, the steam locomotive driver's cab and its equipment, provides a fascinating study. Until the last days of BR steam in the mid-1960s, the basic features of the locomotive footplate were little different from those of the 1840s. The driver still had his place to the rear of the bulk of his machine, a position from which he might not always get the best view of the line-side signals. The skill of the drivers, acquired from long experience, enabled them to overcome many of the difficult working conditions which confronted them every time they climbed up into the cab and took their place among the levers, valves, wheels and pipes and the few gauges which, along with extremes of heat and cold, of vibration, lurching, pounding, smoke and steam, and coal dust, made up the control position. This is the railway equivalent of the ship's bridge, of the truck driver's cab and of the aircraft flight-deck. But none of these control positions is anything like the cab of a steam locomotive.

Some might ask why write a book about a disaster which happened twenty-five years ago? Surely, the circumstances in which we now live and travel have changed so much that no lessons can be learnt with which to study today's railways? Is it not better to leave well enough alone and not dig up facts and reminiscences from a past age, however great the effect of the accident on people and on the events of the time? One answer is, perhaps, curiosity. I suggest there is a need to look at what happened, a need to understand more fully the circumstances of the disaster and to review the causes and effects in the brilliant light of hindsight, to survey the developments in rail safety technology in the succeeding quarter century, and to pose the question 'could it happen again?' It will also serve I hope as a contribution to the history of both technology and industrial archaeology.

My research for this book started in Harrow because this seemed to me to be the most logical place. The town's Civic Centre, which did not exist in 1952, includes a spacious reference library and there among the archives for that part of the county of Middlesex were two buff envelopes of cuttings and photographs. Just two packets of information out of hundreds which recorded events, people and plans from the earliest records of the scattered villages which over the years merged together to form the present borough. One event on one day in 1952 took up only a small space in the history of man, but the contents of the two envelopes left the reader in no doubt about the effects of the accident on the local community at the time, especially as some of those killed or injured came from the district. Many of those who were involved or took part in the rescue work must be still alive. Should they be asked to recount their experiences? Would the disaster have been averted had the automatic warning system (AWS) been

8

in use at the time? These and many other questions came to mind when reading the accounts of the day and the week of anxious rescue work which found not the fifty or so bodies reported in the mid-day papers of 8 October, but more, and more, until a total of 112 was reached, 112 to set alongside the assumed 215 in that other great double collision at Quintinshill in 1915, which had long stood at the top of the list of major British railway accidents.

The records of the double collision were studied against the background of 5000 horsepower electric locomotives hurtling their trains at 100mph through the scene of the disaster of over twenty years before. The same station platforms and buildings could be seen from the windows of the library, and anyone researching through the yellowing newspapers and the stark black and white photographs could hardly fail to gain some rapport with the events of 8 October 1952, one of the first major disasters to be brought home to a nation so vividly by the live reporting of a BBC television news team as rescue was under way.

1

8 October 1952

The sun was just breaking through the overnight mist and fog as 322 people converged on Harrow & Wealdstone station, passed through the ticket barriers on each side of the station, went over the footbridge, down on to Platform 4 and boarded the Tring–Euston local, which had come up the slow line, passed through the crossover to the north of the station and on to the up fast line. The train was already well filled when it drew alongside the platform around 08.17, seven minutes late, and there was much hesitation and running back and forth by businessmen and office workers as they tried to find a vacant seat or even a compartment with only a few standing. The guard waved some towards his brake compartment in the seventh of the nine coaches. As they elbowed their way to a seat or to make room to stand, some grumbled about over-crowded trains, but most who boarded at Harrow were still prepared to put up with some discomfort because the train would run non-stop to Euston in about fifteen minutes. Most of the 800 passengers who were already in the train or had just pushed their way in, were familiar with the sights and the sounds of this busy main line and few gave much thought to the increasing noise of an approaching train. 'Must be that northbound express which passes us about this time.' 'Can't be. The sound seems to come from behind us.' In a whirl of violently assaulted senses those who were not instantly killed

or stunned in the collision, as steel crumpled and wood splintered and the transverse seats scythed through limbs or closed
like traps, may have heard the sound of yet another train
thundering into the station and within a few seconds they had
to survive a second collision.

September 1952 was dull and colder than the average for
the time of the year and the low temperatures persisted into
the beginning of October, with more rain than usual in the south-
east. On 5 October an anti-cyclone over the Atlantic extended
a ridge of high pressure over the British Isles which moved
southward over the Midlands and southern counties of England.
By 8 October the centre of the high pressure area had moved
eastward and was over the southern part of Ireland. The
more usual succession of rain and wind producing cyclonic
weather patterns, which streamed in from the Atlantic, was
pushed towards the north so that over Southern England the
cold and rain gave way to clear skies and sunshine. This
weather was an important factor in the chain of circumstances
leading up to 08.19 on 8 October, possibly the most important
of all. Unfortunately the weather is something over which man
has no control. Rain or fine, mist or clear, are conditions
which chance casts upon every scene.

In Britain the weather, as opposed to the climate, has been
for all time an acceptable subject of conversation. The oft
quoted insularity of Britons is true only if the subject of the
weather is discounted. I use the word weather rather than
climate because it is the hourly changes which are such a
feature of this country's environment. The succession of frontal
systems, which stream generally eastward across these islands,
move at about 30mph and as they usually extend for about
100 miles from leading edge to tail are three or four hours in
passing, which is one reason why a bright morning often
turns grey, overcast and wet by midday. At certain times of
the year the stream of whirling cyclonic lows is pushed further
to the north and then Britain has clear night skies and, as the

land loses warmth by radiation out into space, low temperatures. By dawn or earlier, the moisture in the air will condense
into mists and fogs which persist until dispersed by wind, or
the warmth of the rising sun. The often random sequence of
weather conditions has not only imposed itself on the lives of
the British but has had a considerable influence on the equipment and methods of operating their railways. In other parts
of the world weather conditions are far more predictable so
that the arrival date and the duration of fog, wet or dry periods
can be anticipated within a day or two.

Although the combination of sun and mist, which replaced
the night fogs after dawn, was not unexpected at the time of
the year no one could be certain about visibility because much
depended on localised conditions. Looking from Harrow northward along the tracks towards Headstone Lane the visibility
varied, but at about 08.10 on the day of the accident averaged
200yd. In the other direction, that is southerly, the sun at this
time was, according to the stationmaster at Harrow, just above
the blanket of mist. At 08.18 the sun was climbing from the
south-eastern horizon and moving to the right but still direct-
ing its rays north-westward along the 14 ribbons of steel which
formed the seven tracks through Harrow station. Before the
sun's rays could disperse the mist, assisted by a light breeze,
they shone through it to give a diffused atmosphere which
made the sighting of objects more than 200yd away uncertain.
The effect of sunlight on mist, particularly when looking into
the sun, is to change the normal atmospheric perspective so
that the observer becomes less sure of the distance to objects
and is not always able to separate them from their back-
grounds when the usual distinguishing effect of tone and colour
differences are subdued. There was nothing unusual in an
early morning mist at that time of the year and nothing which
caused signalmen and train crews any particular worries, even
though at dawn the mist had been thick enough to be called a
fog, and for Signalman Armitage in Harrow No 1 signalbox to

put into operation 'fog-working', but at 08.10 he reverted to normal working because he could see his 'fog object', of which, more later.

Signalman A. G. Armitage was in immediate charge of all trains through Harrow, with the exception of those on the electric lines. His signalbox was typical of the period with a many-windowed upper operating room with steps and balcony. Inside was a row of signal, point (switch) and detonator (torpedo) levers with gleaming handles on the side adjoining the fast lines; on a long shelf above the levers were the block instruments for both directions on both fast and slow lines, along with the important indicators which showed that the distant signal for the up fast line was working correctly. Telephones, clock and the train register book or log made up some of the other equipment provided for the safety of train movements. The telephones linked the signalman with the boxes to his north (Hatch End), and south (North Wembley), to the stationmaster and to the District Control room to which he reported the visibility conditions, any untoward happenings in his section and the passing times of important trains. In the event of serious delays to traffic the District Control would give him instructions about which trains were to be switched from one line to another. However, as long as train movements were in the scheduled order laid down in the working time-table or in accordance with standing instructions dealing with out-of-schedule running, the control room relied on the experience of the signalmen to keep traffic moving and did not attempt to intervene.

Signalman Armitage was familiar with the pattern of traffic on the main line at that time of the morning. He knew that movements were dominated by the overnight passenger trains from the north which, with the great distances they covered, up to 400 miles or more (Fig 1), were prone to late running because of the cumulative effects of signal checks, late connecting trains and the weather. To his north the succession of

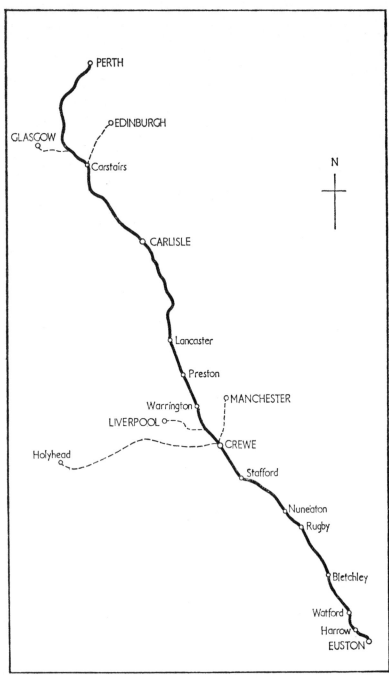

N

Fig 1 : Route of the overnight 20.15 Perth–Euston sleeping-car train, and the West Coast route generally

heavy overnight trains were moving south up the main line. At the same time a stream of steam-hauled commuter trains was coming south from the dormitory suburbs in the Chiltern Hills with such starting points as Northampton, Bletchley and Tring. These trains used both fast and slow lines, depending on paths arranged in the working timetable, to ensure that they kept to time and were not delayed by the overnight expresses from the north. The overnight sleeping-car trains from Scotland were an important part of the country's transport because in 1952 commercial air services were still developing and there were no motorways.

Approaching Harrow from north and south, between 08.00 and 08.18, was a succession of trains on both sets of fast and slow lines (Fig 2). Relevant to the circumstances of the accident are five trains—two southbound overnight sleeping-car expresses from Scotland, the leading one the 22.20 of the previous evening from Glasgow to Euston, followed by the 20.15 Perth–Euston, the 07.31 local from Tring to Euston travelling south, a freight moving north and the northbound 08.00 Euston–Liverpool/Manchester express. The Glasgow–London sleeper was travelling on the up fast line and had steadily lost time after passing Crewe because its driver was treating the foggy conditions with great care. The result of its slow progress was that the following train on the up fast line, the 20.15 Perth–London, gradually closed the 19min gap which had existed at Crewe. By the time the Perth–London train approached the tunnel at Watford it was against adverse signals and was stopped by Watford Tunnel North End signalbox at the home signal for the tunnel section. It had to wait until the Glasgow–London train cleared a 15mph speed-restricted section under repair in the tunnel. Once south of Watford the two expresses gathered speed on the up fast line, swept round the great curving embankment leading to Bushey and entered the final part of the run to the south with about an eight-minute, seven-mile gap between them. As the Glasgow train cleared North

Wembley, the Perth train was passing Bushey station, which meant that it was running slightly faster than the first train.

Somewhere near Apsley the Glasgow sleeper had passed the Tring–Euston local and its load of commuters; some were concerned about the effects of the fog and the possibility of being late into the office, but none expected any serious trouble. The many railway officers in the local train—for the 07.31 from Tring was used by many BR staff from the headquarters offices at Euston—glanced with a professional eye at the fog and mist but, no doubt, quickly went back to reading their newspapers or to musing on the administrative problems of running a railway, problems which they would find listed in their 'in' trays once they reached the London Midland Region office block just across the road from Euston station.

At 07.58 at Harrow signalbox came the single 'call attention' stroke on the block instrument bell for the up fast line. Signalman Armitage replied with one tap on the instrument key. Immediately Signalman Horsfall at Hatch End sent the 4-4-4 special bell code for 'Is line clear for a passenger train not stopping at Willesden?' Checking that all the signal and point levers for the up fast line were in the 'normal' position and, most importantly, that the block instrument pointer showed 'normal', Armitage repeated back the bell code thereby telling Hatch End that the line was clear for the express. At the same time he set his block indicator to 'line clear', which was repeated on the instrument at Hatch End. The up train which he had accepted from Hatch End was, as he knew from his experience with the schedules and the order in which trains were approaching from the north, the Glasgow–London sleeper. When Horsfall received Armitage's reply and his block indicator went to 'line clear' he cleared his signals for the express.

Meanwhile Armitage wrote in the train register that he had accepted the Glasgow train on the up fast at 07.58. However, his signals still stood at danger because he had yet to obtain a

Above: Aerial view of the wreckage of the double collision at Harrow & Weald-stone on 8 October 1952, taken on the afternoon the accident occurred as the rescue operation was under way. *Aerofilms*

Below: Early afternoon as the breakdown cranes start the delicate task of lifting debris. In the foreground lie the remains of Jubilee 4-6-0 *Windward Isles* and the Pacific *Princess Anne* from the Liverpool train. *Keystone*

Above: A general view of Harrow & Wealdstone station looking towards Euston soon after the 1911/12 rebuilding, and taken from the point of the first collision 40 years later. *Locomotive & General Railway Photographs*

Below: Signals at Harrow & Wealdstone related to the accident; on the left is the up fast starting signal No 42, equipped with an intensified light, which it was suggested might have been seen by the driver of the over-running Perth train; on the right, the up slow splitting home signals and, nearer the station, the up fast inner home signal passed at danger by the Perth train. *G M Kichenside*

clear block to the south. After exchanging the appropriate 4-4-4 bell signals with North Wembley and the block indicator for the section ahead to North Wembley showed 'line clear' his up fast advanced starter, until then locked at danger, was electrically released by North Wembley. He then cleared his semaphore stop signals in the order outer home (signal 44), inner home (43), starter (42), and advanced starter (41), which he had to do by the sequential arrangement of the interlocking. (See Fig 3, page 26.) With all four levers in their reverse position he could then pull the up-fast distant lever No 45 and the yellow light of the colour-light signal, over a mile to the north, was replaced by a green. All was thus clear for the Glasgow–London train to pass through Harrow. Armitage however was concerned for the safety of passengers crowding close to the edge of platform 4 so he telephoned the platform staff to warn passengers to move back before the express passed through.

At 08.07 Hatch End sent the two-beat bell code for 'train entering section'. Armitage switched the block indicator to show 'train on line', and entered the fact in the register. Three minutes later the express passed his box and Armitage tapped out the 'train entering section' bell signal to North Wembley. He had replaced the distant signal lever to normal then as the train passed had restored one by one the four red levers back to their normal positions in the frame so restoring all his up fast signals to danger. With all signals for the up fast line restored to the 'on' position Armitage, after calling attention with a single beat on the bell, sent the two-pause-one 'train out of section' bell signal to Hatch End and was able to turn the block indicator for the Hatch End–Harrow section to the 'normal' position at 08.11. Signalman Horsfall, watching his indicator at Hatch End, saw that the block was 'normal' again and therefore he could offer the next train, the Perth–London sleeper, to Harrow, which Armitage accepted.

At the southern end of the main line the 08.00 London–

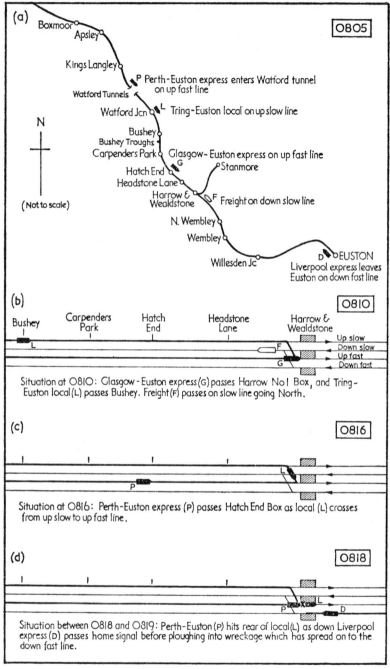

Fig 2 : Time/position diagram of the events leading to the double collision at Harrow & Wealdstone on 8 October 1952

Liverpool and Manchester express left Euston at 08.05, five minutes late because of a minor defect, but, in the chain of circumstances which was forming inexorably from that time onward, it was an appalling misfortune, for had it left on time it might have been clear through Harrow and away to the north by 08.15. As the two locomotives—Jubilee class 4-6-0, No 45637, *Windward Isles*, piloting the unique 4-6-2, No 46202, *Princess Anne*—hauled the 15 coach train up the steep climb of Camden bank and on through Primrose Hill tunnel, little did the crew and passengers know that 15 miles away the 161 ton Pacific No 46242 *City of Glasgow* and its 364 ton train from Perth was just leaving Watford tunnel and starting the fateful last run which would end as an immovable barrier to the London–Liverpool train in the middle of Harrow station. Soon after 08.10 the Liverpool train was offered by North Wembley and accepted by Armitage on the down fast. He in his turn offered it to Hatch End and after acceptance Armitage cleared his down fast line signals.

At 08.07 Armitage had given 'line clear' to Hatch End on the up slow line for the 07.31 local from Tring, which was coming south at about 50mph, with its 2-6-4 tank locomotive No 42389 running bunker first so that the driver was on the right-hand side of the cab in the direction of running, looking out of the cab past the bunker with his controls partly behind him. At Harrow soon after the Glasgow–London sleeper had passed Armitage received the 'train entering section' bell code for the local. The time was now 08.14 and as the northbound freight on the down slow line had cleared the station he was free to reverse the crossover from the up slow to the up fast line so that, in accordance with the schedule, the local could enter Platform 4. With the crossover reversed, the two protecting up fast line home signals were locked in the 'on' or danger position and the up fast line distant was thus displaying a yellow light for caution. As the up fast outer home signal at Harrow was 440yd to the rear of the inner home, Armitage had been correct in accepting the Perth–London train from Hatch End, because the block section was clear up to the outer home signal and for the usual 440yd overlap distance beyond. The crossover was outside this overlap distance. The train register records the time at which the Perth–London train was accepted by Armitage as 08.11.

Three minutes after the Glasgow–London sleeper had rustled the newspapers of the people waiting on the platform for the local, and the express had disappeared under the road bridge to the south leaving a slowly dispersing cloud of steam to add to the mist against the glare of the sun, Armitage received the 'train out of section' bell signal from North Wembley for the Glasgow sleeper. With the local just in the section from Hatch End he offered it forward and it was accepted by North Wembley. However, Armitage did not immediately clear his home signal for the approaching local but waited until the track-circuit indicator showed that it was close to the up slow splitting home signals. Warned by the distant signal at yellow the driver of the local came carefully towards the home signals. As they came in sight through the mist the right-hand, slightly lower, arm was raised to the clear position. He kept the train on the move and it drifted through the crossover on to the up fast line and stopped alongside the crowded No 4 platform at 08.17.

Armitage had kept his up slow home signal on until the last minute in case the driver of the Tring–Euston had forgotten that he was scheduled to cross over to the fast line for the final part of the journey. The London Midland Region was particularly sensitive about the danger of drivers suddenly coming at speed to a home signal set for a low speed divergence just past the signal. At Bourne End in 1945, 15 miles to the north of Harrow on another autumn morning, with the bright sun shining at a low angle into the driver's eyes, an up express was derailed on the crossover from fast to slow line killing 48 passengers and crew. The train then was the same Perth–London sleeper. However, the rules did not specify that trains scheduled to cross from one line to another had to be checked at the protecting home signal.

At 08.17 Armitage heard the distinctive tone of the up fast line bell give two rings; the Perth sleeper had now passed Hatch End and was less than three minutes away, and also must be about to come in sight of the yellow light of his distant signal, or so he assumed. At about this time North Wembley sent him the 'train entering section' bell code for the north-bound Liverpool express on the down fast line. It is clear that Armitage, both in being concerned about the safety of the people who were standing close to the edge of the platform and in ensuring that the speed of the local was sufficiently reduced for the crossover, was acting responsibly. The effect on him when he heard the Perth–London sleeper approaching un-checked with the local standing in its path must have been far greater than the 'astonished' which records his reaction in the Official Report. Here was a man who had operated all the safety equipment correctly and meticulously, suddenly faced with an appalling situation, a situation he must have read about in books, or seen in the cinema. He did not 'freeze' as many would do when faced with the terrible events which were about to happen virtually at his feet. Without hesitation he grabbed the handle of the black-and-white-chevroned lever of the detonator placer for the up fast line and slammed it across the lever-frame. Exploding the detonators beneath its 161 tons, the big Pacific locomotive with its long train of sleeping-cars hurled itself into the local train. To his agitation was added the realisation that there was an express approaching on the down fast, and amid the confusion of events which, like lightning, flashed around him came the dreadful sound of the buzzer announcing that the down express had already reached his home signal, just as he threw the lever back to danger, but just too late for the two drivers of the Liverpool express to see.

23

Nothing he might do could prevent the transformation of three trains into a mound of wreckage, which seemed to explode in the middle of the station. Still attending to his primary duty of ensuring the safety of trains, Armitage sent out the electrifying six-beat 'obstruction danger' bell code to Hatch End and North Wembley for all four main tracks in both directions and then, despite the whirlwind of thoughts in his mind and the scene of carnage outside the windows of his signalbox, he wrote in the register '8.18 Obstruction Danger'. No wonder that when, 10min later, the stationmaster went to the signalbox he found Armitage 'white and shaking', as reaction to the shock of what he saw set in.

Photographs of the clock in the station tower show the hands stopped at 19½min past the hour as mute testimony of the force of the double collision. The tower clock was kept one minute ahead of the master clock, located in the main building of the station, which had been stopped by the shock waves of the two collisions at 08.18½. In the middle of the station there was now a jumbled and jammed mass of coaches out of which began to crawl and stumble the first of those who were alive or not trapped in the wreckage. The cloud of dust and small debris settled, but the roar of steam escaping from the wrecked locomotives continued for some time. The 4-6-0 and the 4-6-2 of the Liverpool express lay on their left sides across the electric lines. A figure lay sprawled on the side of the Pacific for a few moments then, in a daze, struggled upright. It was the fireman of the leading engine, the 4-6-0, who had been thrown out of the cab of his engine, as it hit the wreckage of the first collision, and hurled through the air to land on the side of the second engine. The guard of the Tring–Euston local heaved himself back onto the platform from the slow line whence he had jumped to find his train hardly recognisable as such. The brake compartment, into which he was about to step when he saw the Perth–London bearing down on his train, no longer existed; only the floor and the bent over handbrake column indicated

24

which of the crushed coaches had been his third-brake No 21183, newly built that year.

The Official Report states that the patchy fog contributed to the causes of the collisions but points out that the visibility at Harrow was much more than the minimum laid down in the operating regulations for special fog working. At the same time the Report emphasises that rules and regulations are, of necessity, arbitrary and therefore their effectiveness must depend on the skill and experience of drivers and signalmen. The Absolute Block Regulations, as they applied in those days, permitted the signalman at Harrow to accept a train from Hatch End on the up fast line up to his outer home signal when at danger, and at the same time signal an up train over the crossover from the slow to up fast line. This meant that an up train on the fast line could come within 500yd of another crossing in front of it. As can be seen from Fig 3, the up fast outer home signal stands 440yd out from the inner home which protects the crossover. This quarter mile overlap of the first signal at the end of a section was a minimum distance specified in 1894.

If the fog at Harrow had prevented the signalman from seeing his 'fog object' then he had to introduce 'fog working'. The 'fog object' was the up slow splitting home signals which were 303yd from the signalbox and therefore more than the regulation 200yd, thereby erring by over 100yd on the side of safety. In fog the Harrow signalman was still able to accept a train on the up fast line provided a fog signalman was stationed at the outer-home signal armed with detonators, flags and lamp. A fog signalman was not required at the distant signal, and relevant to the circumstances, this is an important point, because the regulations regarded a multiple-lens colour-light signal to be of sufficient intensity to penetrate fog and therefore the additional protection of a man, armed with detonators and flags, was not needed. If a fog-signalman could not be found for the outer home signal then a train could be accepted on the up fast only if the crossover was set for through running and the

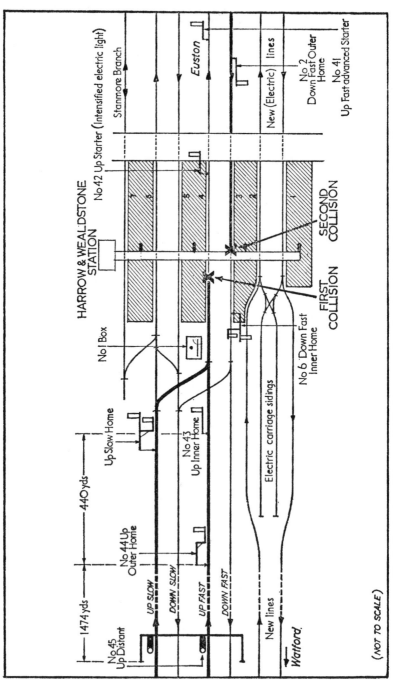

Fig 3 : Track plan of Harrow & Wealdstone station showing the signals relevant to the accident

line was clear for at least 440yd past the *inner* home signal as well.

Fog working was put into operation by Armitage at 06.35 but by 08.10, nine minutes before the disaster, the Harrow signalman reverted to normal working because he could clearly see his 'fog object'. Confirmation of these times came not only from the signalbox register but also from the log of the District Control room. In contrast to the visibility at Harrow, the signalmen at Hatch End and North Wembley had not found it necessary to introduce fog working. Yet, four miles to the north at Bushey the fog became thicker after 07.00. These variations, within less than ten miles, emphasise the patchy nature of the fog.

The Official Report includes an account by the driver of the local train of the circumstances leading up to the collision. His observations of the track and signals approaching Harrow were important to the inquiry because the visibility conditions and the extent to which signals could be seen, applied also to the driver of the Perth–London express. The driver of tank engine No 42389 said the fog was 'patchy'; it had been bad at Tring, clearer through Watford and on the approach to Bushey, but thickened near Carpenders Park and Headstone Lane. He saw the up slow distant at a range of 50yd; this, like the distant for the up fast line, was a multiple-lens colour-light type and carried on the same signal bridge. He did not notice the fast line signal which was about 15ft to his right. His vital comments on visibility on the approach to Harrow included the statement: 'hazy rather than foggy with the sun breaking through and a good deal clearer close to the station that at the distant signal'. As his train ran through the crossover and on to the up fast line the intensified green light of the starting signal stood out clearly against the overbridge at the south end of the platform.

The many photographs which were taken of the wreckage, some of which are reproduced, convey better than any words the terrible destructive power of a colliding train, especially when the engine doing the most damage is one of the largest types of Pacific locomotive in Britain. The coaches lie at awkward angles to each other, their ends flattened, some without roofs and the last three coaches of the local train dissolved into a compressed mass of wreckage, with sets of bogies jumbled in one heap under the mound of debris.

Perhaps, the most remarkable photograph in the archives is that of the locomotive *City of Glasgow*, No 46242, when it had been exposed to view after the wreckage it had caused had been lifted clear. It stands like a battered prizefighter with its smokebox crushed back as far as the front tube-plate of the boiler. Yet it was rebuilt and returned to service. On all sides there remains a carpet of small debris many inches thick.

The loss of 112 lives is an appalling figure, yet the first impression gained from looking at the photographs is that here was a disaster in which, surely, at least 200 must have perished? I draw attention to the pictures of the scene at Harrow at this early stage because they help to make clearer many of the descriptions of events which, twenty-five years later, have been reconstructed from contemporary accounts. The photographs of the other locomotives, *Princess Anne* and *Windward Isles*, also convey vividly the destructive forces released when a heavy train, running close to 60mph, is brought to a stop within a few yards. The Stanier Jubilee 4-6-0 *Windward Isles*, piloting the Pacific *Princess Anne*, on the down Liverpool express, was photographed after it had been re-railed. Instead of being 40ft from front to cab it is only 28ft; the front end, including the heavy cylinder castings as well as much of the smokebox, footplate and cab have been swept away by the impact as it hit *City of Glasgow*, mounted the platform to the left of the line and then toppled on to its side; sliding and dragging or being pushed by the second locomotive. For both *Windward Isles* and *Princess Anne* this had been their last journey since they were too badly damaged to be repaired and were cut up.

In the history of accidents and great disasters on land, sea and in the air there are hundreds of stories of lucky and remarkable escapes. Shipwrecked sailors washed ashore half-drowned following the loss of a ship on a rocky shore, the airline passenger who is hurled clear of an exploding aircraft, and the sensational escapes of passengers and crew in the R101 and Hindenburg airship crashes who literally walked away from death. Harrow 1952 was no exception in the history of remarkable escapes from death or serious injury. There were many in that accident who owed their lives to chance circumstances of time and location, as within less than a minute an orderly arrangement of three trains was smashed into a pile of wreckage.

The *Harrow Observer and Gazette* for 16 October 1952 published a number of first hand accounts of the double collision. One of the more descriptive, and one which was concerned with a lucky escape was that of Mr Arnold, for he was probably nearer to the growing mound of wreckage than anyone else who survived. He was manager of Wymans bookstall, which stood at the foot of the stairs leading from the overbridge to Platforms 2 and 3:

I was at my bookstall and a paper happened to blow out and go as far as the stairs of the footbridge. I had just got there and picked it up and glanced at the 08.11 (Tring–Euston) on the up fast line when it happened . . . passengers were packed and standing in the brake van . . . I had just heard the whistle for the train to proceed but before it could do so, looking down the line I saw the Perth express coming in . . . It crashed into the back of the stationary train and there was an awful explosion . . . I saw a twisted mass of steel carriages and engine lift about thirty feet into the air and it was gradually crawling towards me. It could not seem to get any higher and was cascading and falling towards me. I thought 'This is the end'. I happened to glance behind me and then I saw those two huge engines of the Manchester (Liverpool) express. They were passing within a yard of me . . . they buried themselves in it (the wreckage) as if it were a lump of dough . . . they went through it . . . after it was all over

I was still standing there and there was iron and glass and all sorts of things landing all round me.

In a few hundred words one eyewitness described his lucky escape and at the same time gave a graphic description of the disaster which took place literally at his feet. From the photograph in the *Harrow Observer and Gazette* for 16 October, Mr Arnold appears not to have been affected physically by the events which had happened at his feet because he is seen standing amid the wreckage on the very spot he had stood as the engines of the Liverpool express passed him and ploughed into the wreckage of the first collision, just as they leaped across the platform behind the footbridge. Yet who can tell what the longer term effects are on someone right in the middle of such an appalling disaster.

The guard of the local train, when giving his evidence, told the Inquiry that when the train stopped at Platform 4 he walked forward and, on seeing that many passengers could not crowd into the overfull compartments, he gave them permission to get into his brake van which was part of the seventh coach of the local. He then walked back along his train to check that the doors of the last two coaches were shut and he was just about to walk forward again to his van and give the starting signal when he heard the sound of a train approaching from the north. He turned and saw the front of a big Pacific bearing down on his train. That sight was too much for anyone: he jumped over the platform edge and took shelter on the down slow line, until the dreadful sounds of the two collisions had died away. He scrambled up on to the platform and into a world which in the space of a few seconds had been transformed. The last four coaches of his train were not there; instead was a mountain of debris that had once been part of three trains.

What of the passengers on the 07.31 from Tring?

Suddenly we heard a train coming up fast behind us and we were struck violently. We were thrown to the ground like so many ninepins; we were just picking ourselves up when we heard the Euston–Manchester (Liverpool) train coming through the station in the opposite direction. We knew we were bound to be hit.

That brief statement in the local paper by one of those who escaped death vividly conveys the terrifying experience of those who found themselves still alive but about to go through the horror of a second accident within a few seconds of the first. John Marsden, an artist, recalls the suddenness of the impact of the express with the local train in which he was travelling to work. After the tremendous crash he lost consciousness. When he came to he was in great pain from the crushing weight of debris and bodies and it was some time before he was able to struggle free. He was one of the few survivors from the seventh coach which was partly demolished and crushed between the Pacific locomotive of the Perth–London, which had ploughed under it, and the footbridge and stairway. Of the 18 people in his compartment 6 were dead and some of the others badly injured. The scene of destruction which he saw as he staggered on to the platform is impressed on his mind to this day, in particular the moments before the first rescuers came to help when there were only a few station staff to attend to the trapped and injured. Unlike some of the other survivors, John Marsden does not recall hearing the sound of the approaching express.

The wreckage, which was at least 30ft high and covering an area of about 1500sq yd, presented the rescuers with a dangerous and difficult task. The dead and injured were entangled within twisted steel and splintered wood, and attempts to get to them had to be made with great care to avoid adding to the suffering of the injured. The wrecked coaches had to be torn apart with the rescuers' hands and with small tools. The giant cranes and lifting gear which were rushed to the scene could not be used for some time for fear of starting landslides of wreckage.

In contrast to some other major railway accidents, Harrow occurred in the midst of a busy community and close to hospital, fire and rescue services; those accidents which have taken place far away from a township have always been a particular problem for fire and rescue organisations when they have to travel across difficult country to reach the scene. The Official Report records that the first ambulance and doctor arrived within three minutes of the collisions occurring, closely followed by the Fire Brigade and the Police. The log of the Middlesex Fire Service County Control at North Harrow shows 08.19 as the time the first emergency call was received. From that time on a stream of ambulances, doctors, nurses, firemen and police arrived as soon as it was realised that this was a major disaster. Among the many organisations which rendered medical attention to the injured as they lay in rows on the platform or were still trapped in the wreckage, was a medical unit from the United States Air Force. Col Eugene Coler, Chief Air Surgeon of the 7th Air Division of the USAF, was congratulated later on the generous assistance given by his medical teams and by the special efforts the USAF made to ensure an adequate supply of blood plasma.

Among the many railway officials who were in the local train and who survived the accident were F. W. Abraham, LMR Motive Power Superintendent, L. Rowlands of the operating superintendent's department and S. Williams, the Signal & Telecommunications Engineer. Although badly shaken by their experience and knowing that many of their friends from head-quarters were dead or injured, they immediately set about organising the rescuers, setting up communications and advising other departments of what was needed and what had to be done. With all tracks through Harrow blocked, the country's premier line was strangled at its southern end.

The danger of fire, as in other extensive railway accidents, is always present in the wreckage, but at Harrow, with the fire brigade immediately on hand, the few small fires which started were quickly smothered. Had they not been then the great mound of wreckage, much of which was wood, might have finished up as a heap of ashes, as at Quintinshill 1915. The gas cylinders, yes gas, of the kitchen car of the Liverpool train had their valves broken off which released a cloud of inflammable vapour at the very heart of the wreckage. Having dealt with the small fires and laid their hoses to strategic points to protect the wreckage, particularly while cutting gear was being used, the firemen were able to give their expert attention to the problems of reaching people caught among the twisted frames, splintered coach bodies and dislodged transverse seats. Everyone wanted to help. There were so many willing hands that for their own safety they had to be restrained to stand aside and let the trained gangs do the more hazardous and delicate tasks of probing the wreckage and of making sure that the debris did not topple so adding to the suffering of those trapped and waiting to be rescued from under layers of wreckage.

While those at the station extricated the injured and gave first aid, hospitals in the area were coping with a steady stream of injured for whom beds had to be found and operating schedules quickly changed to deal with those cases whose lives depended on immediate surgery.

All the voluntary services, such as the WRVS and Salvation Army, clergy, and engineering firms in the district, who lent lifting and cutting equipment, made an immediate response and were able not only to help directly with rescuing and looking after the injured and shocked before they were taken to hospital but, of equal importance, they sustained those who were pushing, pulling, wrenching, cutting and squirming their way towards the trapped and injured. Anne Lee, to mention just one among many, a fifteen-year-old student nurse, worked for twenty-two hours without rest until she collapsed from exhaustion. At the hospital to which she was taken it was assumed that she was another casualty of the accident; in a way she was. Six men were also taken to hospital suffering from exhaustion having worked all day. They were aware only of the desperate need to reach those who might still be alive in

33

the wreckage, so that a whole day passed of unceasing heaving, tearing at and probing the tangle of steel and wood with jagged slivers of glass and splinters of wood an ever present hazard. The only respite for many throughout the day—and the night which followed—were the few moments when all work was stopped so that they could listen for sounds of anyone still alive deep inside the heap of wreckage.

On the second day the cranes were still lifting coaches clear, but a point was reached when it no longer became safe for the rescuers to lift and pull at the crushed coaches lest they further endanger those who might still be alive but trapped and unable to call out.

Volunteers offered to risk their lives and go into a 'tunnel of death', as the local paper described it, which had been bored through the main part of the wreckage, with over 100 tons of debris piled on top. Even by the third day the main part of the wreckage was still over 75ft long and 30ft high. All great disasters bring out the superhuman and selfless effort on the part of rescuers and Harrow was no exception. In many ways it required one of the longest and most dangerous mass rescue operations of any British railway accident, only equalled in more recent times by the Moorgate tunnel wall collision in 1975.

During the rescue operation and the clearance of debris all tracks through the station, including the electric lines on the west side, were closed to all movements except breakdown trains, and it was not until a week later that normal working on all lines was possible. In this respect Harrow will always be remembered by those who operated the London Midland Region main line as one of the most traffic-disorganising collisions in the history of the West Coast route. In contrast, at Quintinshill 1915, once the fires had died down, having consumed all but the underframes and bogies of the wrecked coaches and the coal wagons in the siding, the clearing up work did not take very long and trains were soon on the move again.

Above: One of the LMS Coronation class Pacifics, No 6220 *Coronation*, similar to No 46242 *City of Glasgow* and photographed at Headstone Lane leaving the curve by Harrow up distant signal. *C R L Coles*

Right: The controls of an LMS Coronation Pacific. Beneath the left-hand front spectacle window is the reversing lever, to the right of the same window, level with its bottom edge, is the brake handle, and the long lever inclined down in the centre of the cab above the firebox door is the regulator. The driver's position is on the left. *National Railway Museum*

Above: The train engine of the down Liverpool/Manchester express in the accident, No 46202 *Princess Anne*, seen here on an earlier run approaching Harrow having just passed the down outer home signal. *C R L Coles*

Below: A Jubilee class 4-6-0, this one No 45734, but similar to 45637 *Windward Isles*, the leading engine of the down Liverpool and Manchester train in the accident. This photograph shows 45734 on an up train at the exact point of the first collision on 8 October 1952. *C R L Coles*

Breakdown trains with heavy lifting cranes had hurried to Harrow as soon as paths could be found along a main line choked with trains. For example, the Rugby breakdown train did not get to the scene of the disaster until midday. On the next day one of the large cranes was disabled and had to be replaced by the Western Region's crane from Old Oak Common, which travelled from Acton Wells to Willesden to reach the West Coast main line.

Once all the bodies had been recovered from the wreckage the work of clearing the main part proceeded rapidly but not until a week after the accident was the *Harrow Observer and Gazette* able to report:

> Remarkably little trace of the dreadful calamity remained . . . The path taken by the two locomotives of the Liverpool train across the platforms was still marked by torn-up paving stones.

Looking back at the scene by reading contemporary reports and by studying the many photographs published of the wrecked trains and station, and above all the comments of the people who strove hard to rescue the trapped and injured, it is very apparent that the smooth way in which all the different rescue and assistance organisations fitted themselves to the various tasks owed much to training and tradition built up by six years of war. Although the War had ended seven years before, most of the nation's rescue and assistance services were still strongly supported and they retained the efficiency they had acquired from coping with the effects of heavy air raids. Today many of the organisations which did such valuable work at the scene of the disaster have either been dispersed or reduced in size, and it is only in very recent times that thought has been given to the need to establish special rescue groups able to get to the scene of a major disaster quickly and with the training and equipment needed to tackle anything from a railway accident to a chemical works explosion.

On the Sunday following the disaster the repair gangs

paused in their labours at mid day to join in a private service of prayer which had been arranged by the widows of the driver and fireman of the Perth–London express. A wreath of pink and white carnations was laid on the track. At this simple act of remembrance and wherever people gathered to discuss the disaster, arose the persistent question: 'How did all this happen?'

2

Harrow and its railways

Harrow has a place in railway history right from the start of trunk railway development, for the London & Birmingham Railway, the first planned long-distance railway in Britain, provided a station there on the opening of the first section of line from Euston to Boxmoor in 1837. Indeed until 1844, Harrow, with a population of about 4000, was the first station out of Euston after Chalk Farm, a distance of just over 10 miles. The main line of the London & Birmingham, precursor of the mighty London & North Western (LNWR), was planned in 1823, received the sanction of Parliament in 1833, and completed in 1838, only eight years after the opening of the Liverpool & Manchester. Since then, Harrow has expanded as the L&BR developed into the LNWR in 1846, and then into the London Midland & Scottish Railway (LMS) in 1923, and as the environs of London were extended northwestward across the hills and fields of the county of Middlesex.

The London & Birmingham was blessed from its inception because it was a Stephenson line and, therefore, regarded with much favour by the financial houses of the day. In the eight years from the opening of the Liverpool & Manchester much had been learnt, mostly from hard experience, about the design and running of a railway, so that for its time the L&B represented all that was best in high-speed land transport. Above all, it was the first trunk route completed out of London towards the industry of the Midlands and North, trunk because with its eventual end-on connection with the Lancaster & Preston and on over the Lancaster & Carlisle railways it took the traveller northward as far as the Scottish border. In 1846 the L&B, the Grand Junction and the Liverpool & Manchester were amalgamated to form the LNWR, the 'Premier Line', 'The Largest Joint Stock Corporation in the World'.

Such was the progress with railway building that by 1848 the West Coast route ran, uninterrupted, for 400 miles from London to Glasgow and Edinburgh. In those times Harrow was an intermediate station, so that the majority of trains ran through non-stop and only a few semi-fast or all-stations trains called at the little station near the few houses which clustered alongside the road where it crossed the railway.

From Euston, the line made its way up the steep, cable-worked, bank to Camden, where ascending, down (north-bound), trains were taken over from the cable by locomotives, and, in the descending direction, the point at which the engines of up trains were detached to allow the coaches to run unaided down the incline into the terminus. The cable-worked incline lasted from 1837 to 1844, when engines were deemed to be sufficiently powerful to haul trains up the climb from Euston station. Past the Camden engine sheds at the top of the bank the tracks turned westward, through the tunnel beneath Primrose Hill and out to Willesden where a junction was to have been made with Brunel's Great Western so that both companies might share Euston as their London terminus. It was not to be and although the Great Western came within a cemetery width, it turned towards Paddington while in the opposite direction the L&B turned away northwestward without making direct connection.

From what is now Willesden Junction the railway curved right and strode across fields and streams and, ignoring the few scattered hamlets of the Middlesex farmlands, aimed to the east side of the conical hill at Harrow. Its sights were set firmly on Watford and on even more important places on the way to Birmingham.

At the point where a long, gentle left-hand curve, which took the line back to its intended heading, ended, and a generally straight alignment started towards Bushey, the L&B built its Harrow station. It was located as a compromise between the shortest distance a crow could fly across the often waterlogged fields at the foot of the hill and a convenient road crossed by the railway. The contract for building the station was awarded to a Pimlico firm and a contemporary account is given in Roscoe's *London and Birmingham Railway*:

> The Harrow station is a neat brick building, with an enclosure in front where passengers who intend to go by the next train may walk about at leisure after booking their places: or, if they prefer, to repose themselves within doors commodious waiting rooms are provided.

Roscoe might have added a note to the effect that the L&B was not very keen on stopping its trains at Harrow. However, some did stop and Felix Summerley's *Pleasure Excursions* of 1846 included a day trip to Harrow and back, starting at Euston and completing the double journey and the tour of Harrow School, within three hours.

The original station was rebuilt in 1848, and by 1850 considerable building of residential roads and houses had started on both sides of the railway. This area was referred to in contemporary accounts as Harrow New Town, a title not perpetuated. Even the name of Wealdstone is missing from many accounts of the time and the cluster of houses close to the station was known as Station End.

When the railway was the only form of fast long-distance transport in the 1850s, each station tended to polarise commercial and residential building within a radius of a few miles. The original village of Harrow-on-the-Hill retained its importance for many years but gradually a new commercial centre began to expand around the hamlet of Greenhill about half way between the New Town and the Hill. Gradually, this became the heart of Harrow, and when the Metropolitan Railway was extended in 1880 from Kingsbury its line was carried in a cutting at the foot of the high ground between the LNWR station area and the Hill, thereby giving the town a suburban railway station right in the commercial centre. Moreover, there was now a shorter direct route into the City of London, without the dog-leg of the LNWR route (Fig 4).

The original L&B station, by now owned by the LNWR, was rebuilt for the second time in 1860 and again in 1892 as the number of tracks was increased from the original pair to cope with heavier traffic, most of which was still long distance rather than suburban. An up goods line was laid between Watford and Primrose Hill in 1858 and by 1875 four tracks were laid through Harrow. The fast lines were given a new formation on the west side of the station while the original L&B pair of tracks became the slow or goods lines.

In his *London Railway History* H. P. White points out that although the LNWR played such an important part in the economy of Britain, of all the railways which radiated from London it probably had the least direct influence upon the nineteenth-century growth of the capital. The LNWR was interested only in long-distance traffic and its connections with, and interests in, the North London and the North and South Western Junction railways were only for the opportunities they gave for generating through traffic. Not until the twentieth century did the LNWR awake to the need and advantages of suburban trains to the south of Watford.

In the 1850s the LNWR tried to encourage development around Harrow by offering free season tickets valid for 15 years. This, by present standards, was both a generous and a determined effort to capture a new generation of commuters, but train services were not sufficiently attractive and the meadows between Acton Lane (later Willesden) and Harrow remained unspoiled by the rows of villas and terrace houses

42

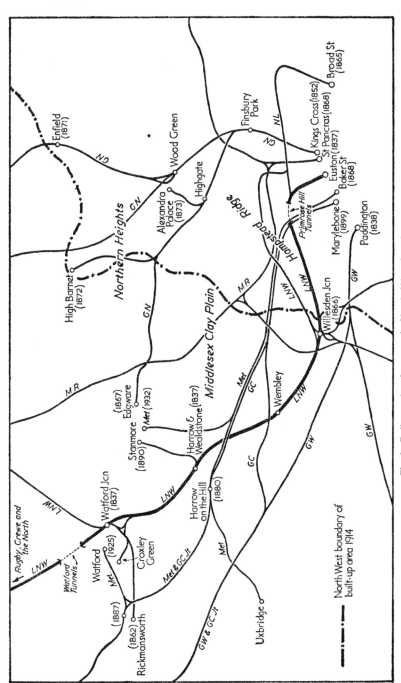

Fig 4: Railway development in North-West London

Enfield (1871)
Wood Green
Finsbury Park
Broad St (1865)
Kings Cross (1852)
St Pancras (1868)
Euston (1837)
Baker St (1868)
Marylebone (1899)
Paddington (1838)
Highgate
Alexandra Palace (1873)
Northern Heights
GN
NL
GN
Primrose Hill Tunnels
Hampstead Ridge
LNW
High Barnet (1872)
GN
Middlesex Clay Plain
MR
Willesden Jcn (1866)
LNW
GW
MR
Stanmore (1890)
Edgware (1867)
Met (1932)
Harrow & Wealdstone (1837)
Met
GC
Wembley
LNW
GW
GW
Watford Jcn (1837)
LNW
Harrow on the Hill (1880)
GC
Met
Rugby, Crewe and the North
LNW
Watford Tunnels
LNW
Watford (1925)
Met
Croxley Green
Met & GC Jt
Met
GW & GC Jt
Uxbridge
Rickmansworth (1862)
(1887)

North-West boundary of built-up area 1914

which, by the middle of the century spread along and outward from the network of railways built by the 'southern' companies. Harrow, by then the first station out from Willesden, was over 10 miles from Euston and therefore not really comparable, as the centre of a passenger catchment area, with those suburban centres within five miles of the Euston Road or of the river termini of the southern lines. The clerk, artisan and labourer were forced to live as close as possible to their work and only the more prosperous were able to contemplate both the cost and time of journeys more than about five miles in order to escape the filth and stench, and the crowded and noisy streets of the city.

Dealing more specifically with the Wealdstone district of Harrow, as Trevor May emphasises, the growth to the north of the LNWR station was stimulated by industrial rather than by residential development. Although the growth of Wealdstone was at first slower than that of Greenhill there was a sudden expansion by the 1890s. In 1891 Kodak opened its factory alongside the LNWR line a few hundred yards to the north of the station and by 1900 employed 500 people. In 1895 there was a large printing works and by 1902 there were seven factories and 22 workshops in the urban district. May's detailed study of the growth of Harrow and Wealdstone makes the point that during the early part of this century Wealdstone was predominantly working class. Industrial growth had added little to the passenger traffic of the station.

One event which might have had a serious effect on LNWR suburban traffic in the area was the proposal to extend the street tramway from Sudbury towards Harrow, through Greenhill and on to Wealdstone. The residents of Harrow and Greenhill vigorously opposed the scheme on the grounds that it would lower the value of their property but those of Wealdstone were all for the tramway. The LNWR held its breath during the tramway debate, but when all the shouting had died down it was able to relax in the knowledge that, apart from the

Metropolitan Railway, which had carved its way through the centre of Harrow, it was safe for a few years from competitive transport around Wealdstone.

In the nineteenth century the growth of the London suburbs was governed to a large extent by the nature of the sub-soil. In those places where the great bed of clay on which London was centred was overlaid by a sufficient depth of gravel or sandy ground, suburban towns developed. Until the end of the century, drainage of both rainwater and sewage relied on the presence of free-draining ground, such as gravel or sand, the sub-soil providing wells for drinking water. The route taken by the L&B, as it turned northward after penetrating the Hampstead Ridge, was across the heavy clay of the Middlesex plain, which lay between the high ground of the Northern Heights to the east and the ridge which ran southward from the hill at Harrow. The woods and meadows of this part of Middlesex did not offer attractive building ground for extensive urban housing.

Those few stations which were spaced well apart along the main line out of Euston were served only by infrequent, semi-fast trains. Sudbury (now Wembley) and Harrow witnessed the frequent passage of the Premier Line's fine expresses as they headed for Birmingham, Liverpool, Manchester, Holyhead and Carlisle and other places on the trunk route to the North. Passing Harrow would be such famous trains as the Irish Mail and on occasions the LNWR's splendid royal train would, in accord with the Queen's 'express' command, hasten-her-slowly to and from her Highland home at Balmoral in Scotland. If not the sovereign herself then it was the Queen's time in the mechanism of a carefully regulated clock in the custody of the guard of the down night mail to Ireland via Holyhead. This carried Greenwich Time to Dublin so that the Irish domain might be kept temporally, if not politically, in step with London.

Even as late as 1900 the LNWR still did not operate suburban services comparable in extent and frequency with those of the other companies. With the exception of the inner suburban services between Willesden Junction and Euston and the associated trains of the North London Railway, the main line did not carry a procession of suburban trains like the services operated in and out of St Pancras, King's Cross and especially out of Liverpool Street and the 'river' stations of the LSWR, LBSCR and SECR. As H. P. White emphasises: 'By 1900 suburban traffic was growing in spite of the LNWR, and next year tube (subway) extensions were authorised from Golders Green to Watford.' Obviously, the LNWR had to do something about the combined threats to its potential and existing suburban traffic, from the Metropolitan, the tramways and from the tube railways.

Within six years of the beginning of the new century the LNWR was able to command capital for new works without too much difficulty. Once the plans for additional tracks and works along with provision for electrification out to Watford had been agreed and published it was seen that they were on the grand scale. The 1906 plan provided for an additional pair of tracks alongside the main line north of Willesden Junction. Harrow station was considerably affected by the extensive engineering works needed to make room for the new lines which would carry improved suburban services to and from the North London Railway and to Euston. Electrification would revitalise the West London line service to Earls Court. The plan also provided for the extension of Bakerloo tube trains out as far as Watford once the 'New Line', which became its official title, had been electrified. Electrification would be at 630 volts direct current on the third and fourth rail system. In addition to the construction of the New Line to Watford the LNWR would extend a branch westward from the New Line at Bushey and Watford High Street to tap the western side of Watford at Croxley Green.

The two new tracks for the electric services made an end-on connection with the Bakerloo line at the point at which it came

46

to the surface alongside the LNWR at Queens Park. The new tracks continued through Willesden Junction, using a new set of platforms, and on through Harlesden and Stonebridge Park, still on the up side, ie to the north and east of the main line. At Watford the major engineering works had to be on the down side, ie to the west of the main line, and at some point between the New Line had to be crossed over or under the existing tracks. Sudbury was the chosen location to transfer the New Line under the existing main line, being laid on a right-of-way recovered from land on the west (down) side of the fast lines. The 1906 plans show clearly that on the approach to Harrow from the south there was not going to be room on the west side of the station for the new tracks, and about a mile to the south of the station the fast and the slow lines had to be gradually realigned towards the east so that the New Line could use the road bed of the fast lines and the slow lines occupied new formation on the east side of the station. The result of these changes, when completed, gave the following arrangement of tracks through the station, in order from left to right when looking northward: down electric, up electric, down fast, up fast, down slow and up slow, with one more track on the east side for the Stanmore branch. The fast lines once again were on the alignment of the original L&B tracks in the station. The New Line was opened throughout between Willesden Junction and Watford on 10 February 1913, but south of Willesden only the older lines were at first available for suburban trains (Fig 5).

Electrification of the system was delayed by the onset of World War I and it was not until April 1917 that Bakerloo tube trains were able to operate out as far as Watford and before July 1922 the full LNWR electric service came into use between Watford and Euston and, via Chalk Farm to Broad Street, although earlier, in May 1914, LNWR electric trains worked the West London line south from Willesden Junction to Earls Court. Also from October 1916 LNWR electric services started between Broad Street and Richmond.

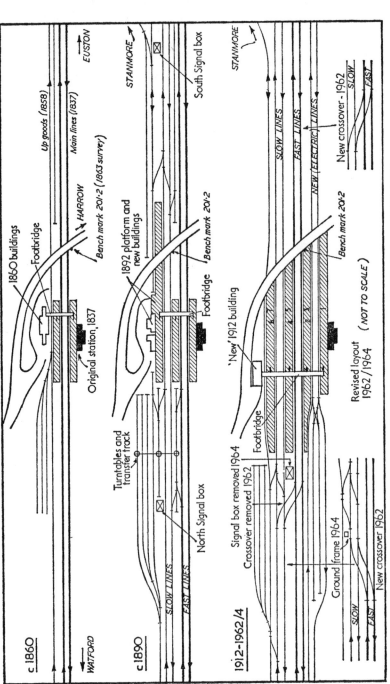

Fig 5 : Development of track layout at Harrow & Wealdstone, 1837–1964

During the construction of the New Line, stations were built at North Wembley, Kenton and Headstone Lane, and another set of platforms was added to the confusing array of offices, public rooms, passage ways, staircases and platforms which added a taste of adventure to the problem of changing trains at Willesden Junction.

From April 1917 when the Bakerloo trains started to serve Harrow, and increasingly from July 1922, when the LNWR and North London 'overground' electric trains added their capacity to the line, Harrow became another transport centre for the urban development which was starting to cover the rolling farmlands which stretched east and west from the slopes of the Hill. At first, the building of rows and rows of semi-detached houses was slow because of the difficult ground which needed considerable preparation before roads and houses could be built on its thick clay. However, once the ground problems had been overcome suburbs spread rapidly around Harrow. Acres of farmland disappeared under concrete and brick. Canons Park, Harrow Weald, Stanmore and Kenton expanded as residential centres in the late 1920s and during the 1930s, when development was even more rapid and widespread. In 1930 I walked through the fields to the west of Edgware looking for the contractors' railway which was preparing the road-bed for the Wembley Park–Stanmore branch of the Metropolitan Railway. From each high point I could look across to the slopes of Harrow Hill with school and church appearing as they did to a farmworker in the middle of the nineteenth century, except that fields and trees had been mostly replaced by 'fields' of red-roofed houses. By 1952 all was concrete and brick, bus and car and the population of Harrow had expanded from 50,000 in 1921 and 97,000 in 1931, to over 220,000.

In general, I have used the name Harrow for the LNWR station rather than the full title of Harrow & Wealdstone. Until 1897 the LNWR timetable for local services referred only to Harrow, and it is not until after that date that the longer

49

title came into use. In the days when there was only the LNWR station, within a mile or so of the growing town, the name Harrow was sufficient, but with urban development around the Hill and the building of the Metropolitan Railway station in 1880, the original station became associated with the area towards the north of the town centre which was Wealdstone.

When the tracks were rearranged as part of the 1906 plan to accommodate the New Line by moving both fast and slow pairs over towards the east side, this needed alterations to the station buildings and the opportunity was taken of making an overall improvement to the passenger amenities. A new station building was erected on the east side to the design of G. Horsley, a pupil of notable Victorian architect Norman Shaw, who did so much to vitalise the design of domestic and public buildings. The west side station buildings, externally at least, still look very much as they must have done to the travellers of a century and more ago. Sir John Betjeman, in his *First and Last Loves*, commented on Harrow station as: '. . . halfway between a bank and a medium sized country house.' The frontage of the station on the up side (east) was designed by H. J. Davis and was featured in the architectural journals of 1912. The 1912 frontage, with its LNWR coat-of-arms, still stands.

Harrow had its share of accidents long before the 1952 disaster. In 1840 an up freight running wrong-line—that is against the normal flow—pulled by two locomotives, came south during single-line working and collided head-on with the engine of a down train which was standing near Harrow station. Two railwaymen were killed. In 1870 there was a more serious accident, involving passengers, when the 5pm out of Euston hit the rear of a coal train. The latter was moving clear of the down line when a coupling broke, stranding the rear part of the train out on the main line. The Harrow signal-man immediately telegraphed back to Wembley Cutting box telling them to hold back the express which was due at about that time. Although the Wembley Cutting signalman kept his home signal at danger, the driver of the express failed to stop. Despite the thick fog and knowing that there was no distant signal for Wembley Cutting, the driver pressed on with apparent recklessness until he was suddenly confronted with a standing train right in his path. There was no time in which to reverse the engines and whistle for brakes. The two locomotives of the express, *Columbine* and *Clyde*, and the 19 coaches crashed with the loss of seven lives including that of the driver of the pilot engine.

The year of 1952 opened with a tragedy when, on 6 February, King George VI died in his sleep after struggling with ill health and worn out after six years of unstinting wartime leadership. After a span of 51 years Britain had a Queen regnant again, and writers of the time talked of a *New Elizabethan Age*. Well a new age it might become but it started with a number of great tragedies as well as disturbing events. It was that year in which John Cobb was killed attempting a new speedboat record on Loch Ness, in which a new fighter aircraft disintegrated above the spectators at the Farnborough Air Show with heavy loss of life among the close-packed crowd but, in contrast, 1952 was a year in which, apart from Harrow, only one passenger was killed in a railway accident. In 1952 there were bitter arguments with the Persian Government over British oil interests and the first signs that a great empire, which had already relinquished control of India, was having to adopt new policies in international affairs. On 30 October 1952 Britain's first atomic bomb was exploded on Monte Bello Island.

'Queen and Judges could please themselves as to whether they went by train or not. But for the mass of Her Majesty's subjects it was fast becoming a case of Hobson's choice. . . .' So wrote W. M. Acworth when describing the railways of 1843 and the rapid demise of the stage and post coaches. In 1952 there was a greater choice: steam and electric trains, bus and private car and the bicycle. The car was just becoming an expected part of a man's property, a parking problem and a threat to the economy of the suburban railways. Many commuters into the centre of London from the outer north-west suburbs still used the steam railway, if there was no alternative such as extended London Transport lines or the Watford–Euston electric services.

It was a time of hope and a time following a period in history during which many ideas and principles had been overthrown, a time, paradoxically, when many things were reviving from the period before the Hitler war; a time when the morning scene at Harrow was still that of 10 or even 20 years before, with the station buildings and furniture and signs reflecting this earlier period. Only the advertisements for products and foods, in place of 1930s and wartime posters, fixed the year. Double-deck buses, upright-bodied saloon cars and the bumblebee-backed Morris, open-top sports cars and cyclists formed the morning rush-hour traffic which flowed along Wealdstone High Street; past the butcher, the baker, the clockmaker; past the coal offices and on past the station driveway. Kodak workers who would have thronged the High Street were at their benches and machines at 07.45 and after 08.00 school children, shop and office workers were queuing for buses or arriving on trains. About every 10 minutes an up express would rumble over the plate-girder bridge to the north of the station and sweep through the array of platforms on which stood ranks of commuters awaiting the next southbound local. In the down direction, northbound trains out of Euston would burst in a flurry of steam and smoke from under the road bridge which spanned the tracks to the south of the station; urged on by engines working hard against the rising gradients towards Watford and the summit at Tring.

The passenger coaches of the fast trains provided examples of both old and new stock. The majority were 1930s-built LMS; occasionally, there were longer-lived LNWR vehicles, even

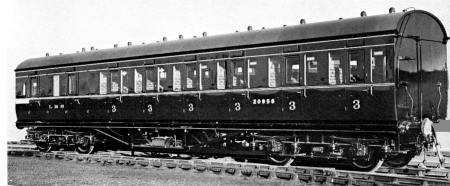

Above: Two of the types of coach which formed the Tring-Euston local on 8 October 1952. At the back was a Midland Railway non-corridor third from the same batch as this one, top. Below it is an LMS standard steel-panelled timber-bodied brake third, similar to the one marshalled seventh in the Tring train. *G M Kichenside; British Railways*

Below: The remains of the Tring train at platform 4; in the centre the bent brake handle column is all that is left above the floor and underframe of the seventh coach. *Public Record Office*

Above: The slow lines were reopened through Harrow two days after the accident but there was still a mass of debris to be cleared from the fast lines. A Liverpool train passes slowly through the station. *Keystone*

Below: The kitchen car of the Liverpool train wedged under one of the footbridge girders, on top of a pile of bogies. The bookstall manager was standing just by the barrow on the left as the two collisions occurred right in front of him. *Public Record Office*

12-wheelers. Some coaches were painted in the British Railways, then standard, red and cream; others still had their livery of LMS maroon with gold lining-out. Semi-fast and local steam trains were usually in the charge of Stanier or Fowler 2-6-4 tank locomotives, which had a reputation for rapid acceleration and fast running between stops. Freight trains were hauled by a variety of LNWR, Midland and LMS locomotive types. On the west side tracks of the station the squat, red tube trains came and went; interspersed were LNWR saloon-type or LMS compartment-type DC electric multiple-units operating the Watford–Euston/Broad Street services. On the east side the Stanmore steam-worked two-coach push-pull affectionately known as 'The Rattler' whistled as it came round the curve from the branch line and alongside Platform 7, many of its passengers intending to cross over to Platform 4 for the next southbound local to Euston.

'More people than usual this morning' commented one of those waiting on Platform 4. 'They must have cancelled a train or it's because this one's seven minutes late' observed his companion. As the local snaked across from slow to fast line and came alongside the platform it had its regular extra two coaches at the back of the rake of seven normally used on the Euston–Bletchley locals. 'Those last two look a bit ancient. Fancy putting those on!' The 300 or so passengers had hardly pushed their way into the train when in a flash the long standing prediction about the 'end of the world' seemed to have come true.

3

Causes and Effects

The circumstances of the double collision at Harrow were made up from a series of chance happenings and compounded in effect by an apparent human failure. The long chain of causes which led up to the double collision, Fig 6, contains the important link of the apparent lack of action on the part of the driver of the Perth–London express when approaching the up fast line distant signal. I use the word apparent when writing about the driver's actions because, as the Official Report concludes, positive evidence of what the driver did or did not do is not available. That the driver failed to reduce speed at the distant signal there is no doubt, but what is far from clear are the reasons for his actions.

The primary link in the safety system was that which existed between signalmen and drivers and the operation of the block system and the lineside signals. Looking first at the block system. What is the block system? This question was even the subject of a letter to *The Times* on 23 January 1877, when two railway critics, with tongues-in-cheek, suggested that it was a method of railway operation whereby one train was used to block a line, then other trains despatched one after another until all were blocked and unable to go forward or go back. The block system is the name for a method of railway working intended to prevent collisions, which has never been defined precisely in Britain. Therefore I hesitate when attempting a

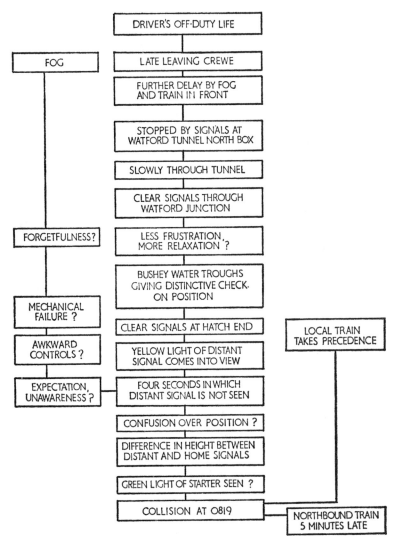

Fig 6 : Chain of causes and effects leading to the disaster

description lest I add yet another incomplete or misleading definition. Nevertheless I think it safe to say that basically it is a system which permits only one train to occupy a section of line at a time. As a principle of safe working it was established over 100 years before Harrow, although it was not until the Railway Regulation Act 1889 that the Board of Trade was empowered to order any railway company it saw fit to adopt the block system on those lines used by passenger trains. The requirement to install a block system was not suddenly imposed on the railways. The principle was long established even if not universally understood in detail. Railway companies were encouraged to adopt a positive method of protecting trains instead of the time interval system as early as 1873 by Section 4 of the Regulation of Railways Act. This required railways to compile an annual report on the progress of installation of the block system as well as a report on the installation of point and signal interlockings. In 1874 a Royal Commission recommended that the Board of Trade be empowered to enforce the adoption of the block system. However there were delays as well as arguments over the definition and it was not until 1889 that the block system was legally enforceable upon the railways of Britain. Yet the definition remained obscure. Even in more recent times the Ministry of Transport, in 1950, referred to the system as 'one which would maintain an adequate space interval between following trains and between converging and crossing trains at junctions'. But what is an adequate space interval? The answer depends on the respondent's own interpretation of the safety of operations.

The importance of a good definition, I suggest, is better understood if the foregoing interpretations are looked at in relation to a block system in which each section is the same length as each train. The requirement that there should only be one train in a section at a time is met, but it does not satisfy the requirement for an adequate space interval between trains. The two requirements were met first by ensuring that until a

58

preceding train had passed the home signal of the box in advance then a following train was not allowed to enter the section which lay between the two signalboxes and which was their joint responsibility. Those companies which adopted a block system in advance of the 1889 legislation considered that they had fulfilled both definitions by providing signals at the entrance to each section and by adopting a standard code of offering and accepting telegraph signals between signalboxes.

The Chief Inspector of Railways, however, was not satisfied with this arrangement and in his annual report of 1875 he criticised the block signalling rules of many companies which allowed a signalman to give 'line-clear' to the box controlling the entrance to a section immediately a train passed his home signal. It can be seen that such a method of working was most unsatisfactory because the preceding train might be held only a few yards past the home signal by a longer than scheduled station stop or by a mishap, so that the following train could then approach the 'protecting' home signal. Under those circumstances the space interval was no greater than the thickness of the signal post.

Many companies were reluctant to introduce operating rules, such as a proper block system with an adequate overlap beyond the home signal, because traffic might be delayed. Many considered that having provided signals it was then the responsibility of the drivers to obey them and theirs was the ultimate and primary responsibility for safety. This was an unfortunate attitude on the part of some railways and it was contrary to the spirit of the safety requirements. Legislators, the Board of Trade and Her Majesty's Inspectors of Railways all preferred to recommend rather than enforce detailed safety regulations, which in themselves were an invitation to evasion, and which were weakened in their intent by attempting to cover the many details of train working and the many variations between types of traffic and the equipments of the various companies. Those answerable to Parliament for safety preferred to be counsellors of safe practices and to rely on the good sense of individual companies when it came to framing operating rules and installing safety equipment.

Without lineside signals to convey information to drivers the block system is incomplete, therefore we need to look at the way in which signals evolved over the years. Lineside signals became, eventually, a most distinguishing feature of Britain's railways because there were few stretches of line along which there was not at least one signal, if not more, every mile. The use of lineside signals, permanently installed, not only replaced the hand and arm signals given by the policemen who governed the passage of trains in the early days, but provided a standard set of indications whose meaning was less likely to be misinterpreted. In the days when policemen stood beside the line they might vary their position from time to time so that a driver might not always be sure where to look. As late as 1858 Lancashire & Yorkshire Railway still protected trains from each other by men stationed at intervals along the whole length of the line.

On 29 April 1858 the Board of Trade made the requirement: 'Signals and distant signals in each direction to be erected.' This was five years after the 5th Report of the Cardwell Committee which had recommended: 'A perfect system of signals . . . would tend much to lessen the danger (want of punctuality and resulting collisions).' The only Act relating to safety, as opposed to recommendations, in that period was the Regulation of Railway Act 1868 (31 & 32 Vict, Ch 119) but this referred not to signals but to the means of communication between passengers and train crews. We have to read on to that milestone of railway legislation, the Regulation of Railways Act 1889. Like the final throwing aside of limitations to the installation of AWS after Harrow 1952, the Act of 1889 was given impetus by a major disaster, at Armagh, on 12 June 1889, in which 78 passengers, mostly children, were killed. We might presume that the introduction of a system of signalling, by which the intentions of those charged with the control of traffic were conveyed to the drivers of trains would have progressed hand-in-hand with the system by which the operation of the signals was controlled. It is one thing to erect lineside signals at intervals, it is another to regulate the manner of their use. The signals installed in the 1850s and 1860s were rarely interlocked with the points or with each other. It was not until 1889 that both interlocking and a standard method of regulating the way in which signals be operated were made mandatory on the railways of this country.

The signalling system in use in 1952 on the main lines of the London Midland Region, Western Division, was that inherited from the LMS which had embarked on an improvement scheme and the installation of colour-light signals in certain areas in the 1930s. Essentially, this was only an interim plan because of financial limitations in peacetime and wartime economies, so that only the main-line distant signals were scheduled for conversion to the multiple-lens colour-light type. Even so, the programme was delayed and by 1941 many distant signals on LMS main lines remained as semaphores. This was the year of a collision at Eccles caused by a driver failing to see both the distant and home signals. Following that accident the LMS announced that it was changing all distant signals on important routes to colour-lights as they fell due for renewal, thus relieving railwaymen of the disagreeable duty of fog signalman during thick weather. Multiple-lens colour-light signals were long in use in Britain before the LMS came to consider their advantages. The first colour-light signals for use in daylight, as opposed to those on underground lines, were used on the Liverpool Overhead Railway in 1920. In one respect the LMS was in advance of other companies in the use of this type of signal. This was the Mirfield speed-signalling system of multiple-lens signals, devised in the early 1930s by A. F. Bound the LMS Signal Engineer; a similar but less complex system was developed for the Euston–Watford DC electric lines.

In general, A. F. Bound's far-sighted signalling schemes, directed at improving the information conveyed to a driver by the lineside signals, came to little because, seemingly, they were not to the liking of other departments in the railway. It has been suggested that the Traffic Department of the LMS in the 1930s kept others, particularly the signal engineers, under its heel and tended to stifle innovation. The mixture of signal types along the main line and on the approach to Harrow in particular may have been a reflection of the unhappy and frustrated signal policies of the pre-war LMS.

The signalling plan, Fig 3, page 26, shows that the Harrow No 1 signalbox controlled five signals for the up fast line, and the facing crossover from the up slow, in addition to the signals and points for all other tracks, but not the electric suburban lines on the west side, which were signalled from Harrow No 2 signalbox. All the stop signals except the platform starter were oil-lit, upper-quadrant semaphores. The starter was also an upper quadrant semaphore but had been equipped with an 'intensified' electric lamp behind the spectacle-plate, in place of the traditional oil lamp, because of the need to distinguish the light against the background of the overbridge and its abutments which spanned the south end of the platform. The official inquiry considered the possibility that this signal, with its light stronger than that of the other signals, might have penetrated the mist and was 'read-through' by the driver of the Perth–London train (Fig 3). This signal was of course clear for the local train standing at the platform.

The Harrow up fast distant signal had a yellow beam focused to give a four degree cone of light, which provided the required intensity for sighting at a distance. Had it been a greater angle there would have been a loss of intensity and the possibility that it might have been confused with the lights of the signals for adjacent tracks. Obviously, the intensity and the direction in which the centre line of the beam of light points, relative to the track, must be a compromise. If the signal could be at the driver's eye-level and the track were straight for at least half a mile on the approach, that would be an ideal arrangement, but when there are adjacent tracks separated by the British standard 'six-foot' there is not always adequate room in which to fit a signal. Therefore with an adjacent track on the driver's side, as at Headstone Lane the up fast distant signal had to be suspended from a signal bridge spanning all four tracks. Fig 7 shows the essential dimensions of the up fast distant signal as well as the distant signal for the up slow line, both carried on the same bridge.

The LMS instructions relating to the sighting of colour-light signals published in April 1936 included the following requirement: 'It is essential that in all cases colour-light signals be fixed as near as possible to the driver's eye, ie always on the left-hand side of the track and at minimum distance from his eye level in a vertical plane.' The track approaching the distant signal was on a long curve to the left of 234 chains radius; this is a curve of just under three miles radius so that the track can be envisaged at that point as being part of a circle nearly six miles in diameter, not a severe curve.

To meet the incompatible factors of a curved track and a straight beam the signal engineer aligned the centre of the cone of light so that it intercepted the near-side rail, that is the driver's side, 50yd out from the signal (Fig 8). Because the beam of light spread out as a four degree cone, the edge of the beam of light intercepted the near-side rail about 600yd out so that the intensity of the light steadily increased from 600yd to 50yd from the signal. At the then line speed limit of 75mph, those 550yd in which the light steadily increased would, given ideal conditions, be in a driver's sight for about 15 seconds. Although the inquiry was not able to give a positive conclusion about the speed of the Perth train between Hatch End and Harrow it was unlikely to have been 75mph, more like 55mph. Therefore in ideal conditions the distant signal might have been in view for nearly 20 seconds. However, as the Official Report points out,

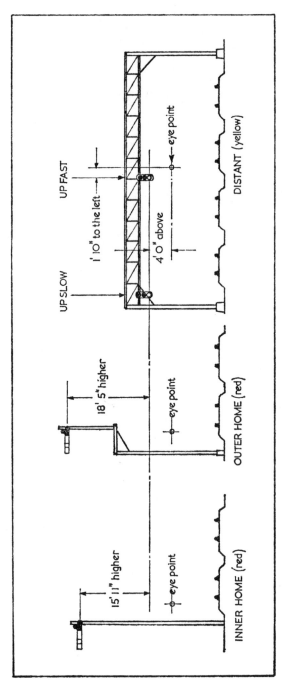

Fig 7 : Up fast line signals at Harrow in relation to driver's eye point

the visibility south of Hatch End might have been no more than 100yd, which meant that the signal was in the driver's sight for only about four seconds.

The up fast distant was 1474yd out from the outer home, in other words just under a mile and therefore giving adequate braking distance, even if a driver did not apply the brakes until actually passing the signal at the 75mph maximum then permitted on the Western Division of the LMR. The distant signal was one of those semaphores which had been replaced by a multiple-lens type. If had three lenses even though in signalling terms only two aspects were needed; when clear or 'off' a single green light indicated that all the stop signals for the up fast line through Harrow were also clear; in the caution or 'on' aspect, it indicated that one or all of the fast line stop signals at Harrow were at danger. Certainly it denoted that a driver must be prepared to stop at the outer home signal. The uppermost of the three lights in the distant was an auxiliary lamp for yellow; the middle lens was for green and the lowest for main yellow. The auxiliary yellow was lit automatically if the main light were to fail.

In Harrow No 1 box, above the lever controlling the distant signal, was a three-aspect indicator from which the signalman could verify that his up fast distant was not only showing the correct aspect but that the filaments of the lamps were intact. If the main yellow were to fail, in addition to the repeater indicator going to the 'no-light' aspect, a loud annunciator sounded and this could be stopped only after the signalman had turned a cancelling switch. When the main yellow of a distant signal failed, the standing instructions required the signalman to stop accepting trains from the box in the rear until the signalman there had been advised of the failure. If the signalman at the previous box was able to see clearly that the auxiliary light of the distant signal for the next box had come into operation then normal block working could be resumed. If the auxiliary light were not visible then all trains had to be

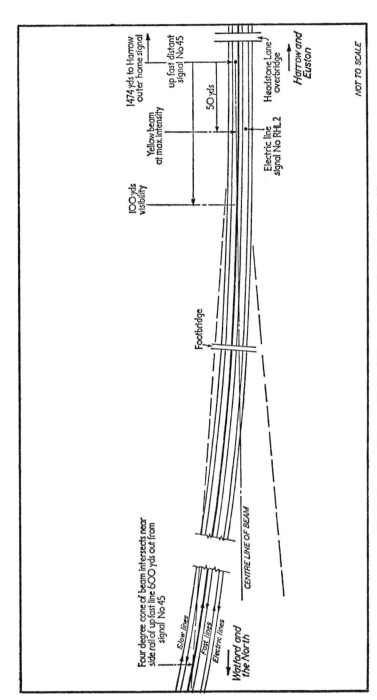

Fig 8 : The coned beam of light of Harrow up fast distant signal No 45

stopped and drivers warned of the failure and told to approach the distant signal and pass it on the assumption that it was showing yellow.

Although the inquiry showed that there was nothing wrong with the distant signal I have deliberately emphasised the importance of the evidence about this signal, because it is a key point in the chain of events leading to the collision and also explains why the illustrations of the signal show three lenses and not just two, as might be expected with a basically two-aspect signal. The provision of two yellow lenses at LMS and London Midland Region colour-light distants arose, in part, from an attempt to adopt a measure of 'speed-signalling' for all main line distant signals, as propounded by Bound. This required a double-yellow aspect to indicate that the next signal —which would be a semaphore—should be passed at restricted speed, possibly because a junction had been set for a diverging route which required a reduction of speed. Because this meaning might be confused with the other meaning of double-yellow on a line with continuous multiple-aspect colour-light signal-ling—be prepared to find the next signal at single-yellow—it was decided after the Bourne End (1945) derailment of the Perth–London sleeper to give up the double-yellow as a 'speed' signal in otherwise semaphore areas. At Bourne End on 30 September 1945 the driver of the Perth–London sleeping-car train might have been confused when he came upon a double-yellow followed by a clear semaphore outer-home and then a set of 'splitting' semaphores with the left-hand signal indicating a low-speed diversion from the fast to the slow line.

There was no doubt that as the 20.15 Perth–London sleeper approached Harrow on 8 October 1952 the distant signal was showing the single-yellow caution aspect and the outer and inner home signals were at danger. This was established to the satisfaction of the inquiry along with all other actions on the part of the signalman intended to prevent an accident. Essentially, the final safety check depended on the driver obeying the stop indication of the outer home signal, having been warned of its danger indication by the single-yellow at the distant signal, 1474yd to the north. Additional safeguards were the detonators which could be placed on the line outside the signalbox in the event of a train overrunning signals. The detonators could be moved into position by the signalman operating lever No 40 and would be kept in position during fog working until an approaching train had been seen to come to a stand at the outer-home signal; if it were then clear for the train to draw forward the replacement of the lever would withdraw the detonators. Moreover, in fog working, the rules stipulated placing of a fog signalman at the outer home signal itself and he would have placed detonators on the rail at that signal when it was at danger. Because fog working was stopped at 08.10 there was no fog signalman and no detonators in position. These 'torpedoes', using the North American term, provided an effective attention-getter in the days before cab-signalling and the automatic warning system (AWS). The detonator placer in the signalbox was of little use in the circumstances of the accident since the detonators were only a few yards behind the local train.

The main line from the north was to the advantage of up trains because it fell for the most part from the summit of Tring with many long stretches of 1 in 335 and 1 in 339, with one longish dip between Watford and Bushey. In steam days, once a train had cleared the summit heading south most of the fireman's work was finished and he could relax. To some extent the driver could also relax because he no longer had to make a precise balance of the controls in order to maintain schedule without, figuratively, breaking the fireman's back or actually running out of coal and water towards the end of the run. Once through the tunnel at Watford an up express could run towards Euston with the reversing gear well linked-up and with the regulator nearly closed. However, despite the less arduous task of driver and fireman, compared with the earlier part of the run to the south from Crewe, they were both still very much concerned with observing signals and even more so if their train was running late because of fog. In itself, fog enjoined extra vigilance, particularly when there was no AWS, with its reassuring ring of the bell at each clear distant signal which Great Western drivers enjoyed.

As the Official Report records, the Perth–London train left Crewe 32min late and 19min behind the 22.20 (Tuesday) out of Glasgow. The fog south of Crewe was thick enough to affect the sighting of signals and the Glasgow–London train began to lose time, which in turn resulted in the Perth train gradually closing the distance until by the time the first train slowed for the 15mph temporary restriction through Watford tunnel, $8\frac{1}{2}$ miles north of Harrow, the second train was in the section behind it between Kings Langley and Watford Tunnel North End signalboxes and had to be held at the home signal controlled by the latter.

By the time the Perth sleeper had been cleared to pass through the tunnel and had emerged on the other side, all signals through Watford Junction were clear, as were those through Bushey and Hatch End. The train was now 82min down on schedule and this alone should have made the driver even more attentive to signals. The fog and the consequent delays to all trains meant that there was more than a chance they would be delayed even further by trains having a higher priority, such as the suburban trains inbound to Euston. The Official Report emphasises this aspect as follows:

> Every endeavour is made to keep these 'residential' services to time. Except in an emergency, the signalmen are not expected to vary the routing laid down in the working time-table, and the residential trains are given precedence over any night expresses from the north which may be running late. This is well known to all the local staff and main-line drivers generally recognise that if they arrive late in the London area at this time of the morning they may expect further delays.

It is as if the driver of the Perth train forgot all about the 'expected' delays if he arrived late from the north and that once

69

clear of Watford tunnel and with all signals off at Watford Junction, Bushey and Hatch End, he assumed, possibly, that the train in front had got well ahead and therefore he would suffer no more delays, at least not until approaching Euston where he was more than likely to be brought to a standstill to wait for an empty platform.

The Chief Inspecting Officer, Lt-Col Wilson, made a special study from the driver's position of the sighting of signals on the approach to Harrow from the north. The Official Report records that the up fast distant came into view at a range of 733yd and the up electric line signals HL4 and RHL2 near Headstone Lane station, when showing green lights, appeared to the right of the up fast yellow. To an ordinary observer and not necessarily to an experienced driver, the yellow light of the distant signal might have been mistaken for the electric line signal but when a train was close to the up fast distant signal there was no doubt about its indication and to which line it referred. Lt-Col Wilson observed that at first the signal light was dull because, as shown in Fig 8, the beam centre-line was only coincident with the track at a point 50yd from the signal. The light improved steadily the closer the engine came toward it until 80yd from the signal it was at full intensity. At that point the green light of the Headstone Lane up electric line platform starting signal, HL2, came into sight ahead, but, as the Official Report emphasises, it was away to the right.

At this critical point in the approach to Harrow did something distract the driver's attention? Was it the distant signal for the up slow over to the left? Had there been no mist, this signal would have come into view at a range of 500yd but it, too, was showing yellow. On the general question whether the driver was confused between signals, the Report emphasises that an experienced driver would not have mistaken one signal for another, even though it acknowledges that a certain degree of care was necessary to avoid distraction by the electric line signals, but no more than that needed by a driver at many other

Top left: The damaged cab of No 46242 *City of Glasgow* which had worked the Perth train; the regulator handle is closed, the brake handle on the left is bent but in the 'on' position, and the broken cock and pipe of the left hand gauge glass is bent down behind the regulator handle. *Public Record Office. Top right:* The front end of *City of Glasgow* after the engine was retrieved from the wreck. It was later rebuilt and put back in service. *Public Record Office. Left:* There was little left of *Windward Isles* as it was lifted from the electric line sidings. *Keystone*

Left: At the time of the Harrow accident BR was about to start trials of a new automatic warning system. Here a steam locomotive is seen with its receiver equipment poised over the track magnets.

Below: The cab equipment of the automatic warning system showing the circular visual indicator, displaying the spoked pattern, denoting the acknowledgement of a caution signal. *British Railways*

places where reliance had to be placed on his experience and knowledge of different signals.

After the accident the lay press and public opinion questioned the action of the signalman in crossing the local train in front of the up express. These comments reflected a lack of understanding of railway operation and, as the Official Report records, no blame was attached to signalman Armitage's actions. However, it is worthwhile looking at the circumstances behind the arrangement of trains which prompted the comments. To do this we have to look at the relationship which existed in those days between signalmen and controllers. Each was both dependent on and independent of the other, according to particular circumstances. If all trains were running on time then the timetable was the controlling factor and this provided a reliable prediction of future events from which signalmen and controllers could get positive guidance. In other words, if all trains were to schedule then the signalmen's actions were routine and the controllers just observers and recorders. It hardly needs emphasising that a railway is just as imperfect as the rest of the world, with both expected and unexpected events interrupting the smooth flow of planned events. The train control system for the main lines of the London Midland Region had been established by the LMS in the late 1920s. The complete region, with the exception of a few lines, was controlled from Divisional and District Control centres. In these centres the staff were able to contact every signalbox, stationmaster, yardmaster, locomotive superintendent and coach shed, key centres as well as outside agencies, such as rescue services, by means of a comprehensive private telephone network. Harrow No 1 signalbox came within the network of Euston District control.

It is important to stress that controllers rarely conducted a running commentary of orders and advice in the same way in which air traffic control is exercised. They acted only when they could see that something was about to go wrong with the smooth timetable running of trains. The routine control of

E   73

trains remained as much as possible within the direct control of the signalmen.

The events of 8 October 1952 provide a good example of the link between controllers and signalmen because at 06.35 the controller for the section which included Harrow saw the light on his control panel come on. Moving the answer key he heard signalman Armitage say 'Fog on 06.35 Harrow'. He noted in his log the fact that visibility was reduced sufficiently for Armitage to have started fog working. He also started to think about the problems which would begin to arise as the night expresses from the North started to converge on London and would have to be fitted in among the scheduled commuter trains. Possibly it was with some relief that the section controller received the 'fog off' message from Harrow No 1 box at 08.10. The busy time was getting under way but at least the fog must be lifting.

The concept of a control room from which the overall running of a geographical area of a railway was supervised, originated on the Midland Railway, was copied by the Lancashire & Yorkshire and because both were constituent companies of the LMS the principle was adopted for all but a few parts of this vast system, which stretched from Poole in the south via the Somerset & Dorset, from Swansea in Wales by the Central Wales line, from Southend in the east, to Thurso in the far north. Centralised traffic control was pioneered by the Midland with an experimental telephone control network at Masborough near Sheffield, in 1907. Initially the Masborough centre was concerned primarily with the regulation of the hours worked by train crews and with arranging relief crews but the success of the scheme encouraged Cecil Paget, the General Superintendent, to extend it to the control of train movements over the most congested sections of the Midland. From 1909 the Midland's centralised control system was expanded to cover all but a few parts of the railway.

When the LMS reorganised the control districts in 1946 into 19 centres the control office at Willesden, which was responsible for traffic between Euston and the boundary with the Bletchley control area, was closed and a new centre opened on the west side of Euston Station. This district control had authority over all movements north as far as the boundary of the new Rugby control area and it also included control of the North London line and the DC electric lines out to Watford.

Along one side of the control room at Euston stretched a track map of the control district on which was marked the positions of signalboxes, stations, sidings, crossovers, water columns and tunnels, along with such important facts relating to each location as the length of sidings and the number of wagons which could be accommodated.

The controllers, who sat at a contiguous line of control desks, one for each section, communicated with signalmen and other operating staff over the comprehensive telephone network which included a number of omnibus circuits whereby a controller could broadcast information to more than one location at a time. On the track diagram in front of each controller there would be special cards to show items of particular interest, such as temporary engineering works, a failed signal or any fact not included in the working timetable. As trains passed selected reporting points, controllers would be given passing times by signalmen which they checked against the graphic schedules on their desks. Controllers kept an eye on special loads, on the working hours of crews and ensured that relief men were ready to take over a train if need be. Other controllers watched over the movements of locomotives and rolling stock to ensure that the most effective use was made of both, and that spare locomotives were available to take over in the event of an engine failing.

Control rooms were not disordered hives of activity. There were no frantic bells and shouted orders and enquiries. The railway was scheduled to operate in an orderly manner so that the controllers were more concerned with anticipating trouble and taking action to lessen the effects of trouble and with taking quick and effective action when disaster struck, as it did at 08.19 on 8 October 1952. Within a few minutes of the first call light flashing on the panel of the section controller for the southern end of the line, and as he listened to the first messages about the double collision, the control room became the nerve centre for redirecting trains on to alternative routes. The controllers worked closely with adjacent district control centres and with the rescue co-ordination centre which had been set up at Harrow & Wealdstone station by S. G. Hearn, operating superintendent of the Region. The control centre had to advise all signalboxes, station and yardmasters and key points of the complete blockage of the main line. An important task was to make sure that the lines were kept open on both sides of the wreckage so that the breakdown trains with their heavy lifting cranes could reach the wreck.

Although the immediate effect of the double collision was to halt all traffic, once the control room had sorted out alternative routes trains started to move again, albeit from unusual stations and over unusual routes. For example, some scheduled Euston departures were operated either out of Paddington or St Pancras, the former using the GWR line to Birmingham, either as far as Leamington and then crossing over to the London Midland line to Coventry or through Snow Hill station (Birmingham) and on to Wolverhampton; trains from St Pancras reached the main line from Euston to the North at Nuneaton. Initially, some trains already waiting to leave Euston or on their way, were diverted from Willesden Junction through the goods lines to Acton Wells Junction. Here the trains were reversed and moved north over the line to Brent Junction on the former Midland main line, then northwards and across from Wigston to Nuneaton to regain their scheduled route. Fig 9 shows some of the alternative routes used during the week following the accident. Services on the DC electric lines terminated at Wembley and at Hatch End, with London Transport buses shuttling passengers between the two points.

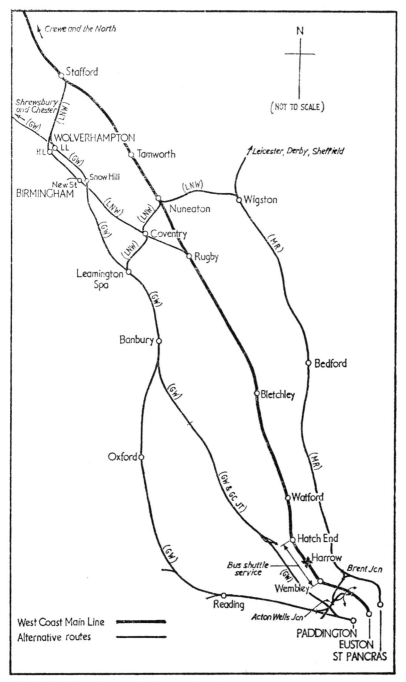

Fig 9: The West Coast main line and the alternative routes used while the line was obstructed at Harrow

4

Man and machine

Each of us is familiar with the equipment of our place of work. For each of us there is a familiar work or control station which might be in a private car, a boat or ship, the flight-deck of a supersonic aircraft, the control panel of a steel mill, margarine plant or just our office desk or kitchen sink. These are the positions at which each of us, at some time in our lives, has to make decisions about what has to be done next in the light of the available information. Between ourselves and the world of commerce, of machines and vehicles there is a boundary across which we make contact and take such control actions as moving a switch, pressing a button, turning a wheel or just writing and typing. From the other side of this boundary flows the information needed to complete a task or to control a machine, for example, the road ahead, the track ahead, the runway, the harbour entrance, an inventory, a letter and even the book from which we get both information and enjoyment. Even electronic boundaries are now familiar to all in the shape of domestic television, the car-park exit and the pocket calculator. This chapter deals with some of the reasons which might have contributed to the failure of the driver of the up Perth express at Harrow either to see or respond to the yellow light of the distant signal. It is not enough to say that he missed the signal. We need to know more about the control interface in the loco-motive cab and the amount of information available from the view ahead, as well as some of the ways in which the driver might or might not have reacted to events.

The photograph on page 35 shows the cab of a Stanier Pacific, similar to the cab of No 46242, *City of Glasgow*. This is the man-machine-interface. The driver's position is on the left with the principal controls arranged so that he can operate them either when standing or when sitting on the hard wooden tip-up seat. The most important group of controls consists of the regulator (throttle), the reverser cut-off wheel, and the control handle of the combined vacuum-steam brake system. The front of the cab is wedge shaped so that the front glass does not reflect any lights in the cab or the strong glare when the firedoor is open.

The forward window, set at an angle, is the only view ahead, other than when the driver cranes his head out of the side window. The view ahead is difficult to describe accurately because there are so many different conditions of visibility and driver's head position to consider. To emphasise this we need only think of the car driver's forward view of the road. This can be described in general terms because the head is usually kept close to one position relative to the windscreen, unless the driver lounges to one side with his elbow out of the window The locomotive driver might be standing, sitting upright in his seat looking forward through the narrow front window, or leaning with most of his head out of the side window. This means that his arc of vision might vary between 20 degrees each side of the view straight ahead to nearly 60 degrees altogether. The Official Report describes how the inspecting officer rode on the footplate of another Pacific to check the visibility of the up fast distant signal. The report does not specify exactly from which point on the footplate the observations were made. Of course, this is rather an academic exercise, particularly when related to all the other possible causes of the accident. Nevertheless, this aspect helps us to appreciate better the sighting task of the driver of a steam locomotive as he

tries to pick-out a signal as soon as possible, with the bulk of
the engine obscuring most of his forward view. The diagram,
Fig 10, shows the narrow field of view through the front window
of an LMS Coronation Pacific approaching a colour-light
signal gantry like the Harrow up distant signals.

There was no evidence available to the inquiry to show
exactly the driver's eye-position at the time when the distant
signal came into his view, although the signalman at Hatch
End recollected that he saw the driver's face through the
spectacle. The spectacle is the small forward window of the cab
and it derives its name from the time when the only protection
from the elements afforded the enginemen was a windscreen
with two circular glass ports which looked like a pair of spec-
tacles. Sitting at the controls of a Coronation class Pacific, the
forward view, as I found from personal observation, is not very
good, either with the head inside the cab or when leaning out
of the side window. The limited forward arcs of vision may not
have been a handicap under the circumstances of 8 October
1952 but they cannot be said with any certainty to have made
the driver's task any easier, particularly if he was not sure
of how far south he was from Bushey. Had he been at the front of
the locomotive, as in an electric train, the much wider area of
vision would have given a far better view of the lineside
features by which he could check on how far forward he had
gone since passing the last signal.

The driver of *City of Glasgow* had landmarks at Hatch End
with the semaphore home and starting signals and the road
overbridge half a mile to the north of the Harrow up distant
and this would have given him a positional check. It is during
the 30 or 40 seconds running southward from Hatch End toward
the distant signal that the driver may not only have misjudged
his exact position, but also the period in which the distant
signal should have come into sight and remained in view for
about four seconds in the 100yd visibility.

As the inquiry emphasised, the distant signal was well

Fig 10 : The field of view of a driver through the front spectacle window approaching a colour-light signal gantry such as the Harrow up distant signals

sighted and had a strong light which a driver attending to the road ahead would hardly have failed to see. If, as the Hatch End signalman testified, the driver was sitting at the controls with his head inside the cab looking forward through the spectacle glass, the restricted angle of view might not have given sufficient time in which to pick-up the beam of the yellow light.

Was the driver distracted? If we consider the conditions in the cab that morning, just as the distant signal came into view through the mist and against the diffused sunlight, and if the cab was suddenly filled with steam and scalding water from a broken pipe or fitting, the bottom gauge-glass cock for example, then it is not difficult to see how the train might have gone by the distant signal while the driver's attention was distracted. Possibly the driver and fireman could have rectified the trouble but in so doing missed the signal and then found they were much too close to Harrow when they came to look forward again. A letter in *The Engineer* of 18 September 1953, from a driver, emphasised that because the signalman at Harrow said he did not see the enginemen of the express as it came into sight did not mean that they were not making superhuman efforts to stop their train. Again in the pages of the *The Engineer*, on 4 September 1953, a correspondent points out that the Official Report, at paragraph 5.3, states: '. . . the two water gauge-glasses were intact, but the drain pipe and cock of the left-hand water gauge had been torn away and must have released some steam and water into the cab'. The gauge referred to can be seen clearly in the photograph on page 71. Could the drain cock have fractured from metal fatigue during the time the train was passing the distant signal?

The letter in *The Engineer* suggested that metal fatigue had weakened the phosphor-bronze cock to an extent that it was likely to fail unexpectedly. With hindsight it is easy to talk about such possibilities. All the same the writer of the letter did not hesitate to voice his concern. It is interesting to note that the metallurgist's report on the examination of the gauge cock was not included as an appendix to the Official Report.

Having missed the signal was the driver then in some doubt about his whereabouts? Had he passed the distant signal? Would it show up in a few more seconds? When it was too late and the outer home signal loomed out of the mist, instead the driver, as the evidence suggests, made a full brake application. The regulator was already closed, or almost closed, and most likely had been since passing Bushey five miles back. Another factor which the inquiry considered could have added to the driver's signal viewing problem was the difference in the heights of the multiple-lens colour-light distant signal and the semaphore home signals.

The up fast line distant signal yellow light (Fig 7, page 64) was 14ft above rail level and 3ft in the vertical plane from the nearside (left) rail of the track. Not only were there differences between the types of signals but their heights above the driver's eye-level varied. This is why the inquiry looked at the possibility that the driver had his attention diverted for a short time, perhaps only a few seconds, and that he then continued to look out for the distant signal with his gaze directed approximately at the 14ft level. With the outer home signal over 15ft higher than the distant it would have come into the driver's view even later than expected. Note how difficult it is to get away from the word 'expected'.

Adding to the driver's problems in sighting signals was the smoke and steam which blows and drifts down and across his forward view, also the possibility mentioned by Lt-Col Wilson that the low sun might have affected the background to the home signals. The sun, $17\frac{1}{2}$ degrees to the left of the straight section between Headstone Lane and Harrow and 9 degrees above the horizon, might well have diffused a misty background.

The problem of the exhaust obscuring the driver's view was aggravated when boilers became much larger and chimneys shorter in the 1920s, also when engines were worked at short cut-offs. Ways had to be found to make the air at the front of a locomotive flow upwards instead of spreading outwards. The top of the smokebox was sometimes flattened to form a wedge; sometimes a system of cowls was arranged around the chimney. Earlier, in 1894, the Jones 4-6-os of the Highland were given an annular casing to the chimney with slots in the forepart so that a draught of air would be induced to form an upward moving sleeve of air around the exhaust to prevent the latter beating down around the cab. Some of the attempts to eliminate the problem were based on wrong assumptions. It was not until more thorough research, using wind tunnels and more importantly, using full-size engines in real conditions, had been completed that it was realised that essentially a smoke 'deflecting' system had to make the air flow close alongside the boiler, filling the low-pressure, turbulent area resulting from the outward spread of air from the flat front of the smokebox. Moreover, the air flow had to counteract a wind blowing across the track, which caused eddies on the lee side of the boiler, into which would be drawn smoke and steam.

One of the most effective cures to the problem were deflector plates fitted on each side of the smokebox, evolved in Germany in the 1920s and found to be both effective and simple. *City of Glasgow* had large side deflector plates intended to prevent the exhaust beating down and obstructing the view ahead, but in certain conditions of wind direction, throttle setting and cut-off they were not always effective. The Official Report records that the engine was running with the throttle closed and blower on, so it was assumed there would have been only a small amount of steam to obscure the driver's view-ahead. Nevertheless, a description of the driver's signal sighting task would be incomplete without mention of the smoke deflecting arrangements, particularly as there was no positive evidence about the setting of the controls or the amount of steam and smoke emitted when passing between Hatch End and Headstone

84

Lane. The chart Fig 6, page 57, is an attempt to show how a number of events, causes and effects came together as the three trains collided in the middle of Harrow & Wealdstone station. Part of the diagram is the chain of events in the driver's life. Not just for a few minutes immediately before the collision of the Perth train with the local, not just the time of the run southward from Crewe, but in the days leading up to 8 October, days on duty and days off duty. The Official Report refers to an investigation of the driver's activities before the fatal run. His home tasks, such as repainting his house with a certain type of paint, which might have affected his health, are in the report, as are comments along with evidence from other railwaymen about his domestic and working life. There was also the post mortem. All were considered when trying to find out why the driver failed to act upon the indication of the distant signal. However, the Official Report does not ascribe any one of these factors as being contributory to the primary cause of the accident, the failure to observe or react to the Yellow of the distant.

The question of how far back and to what detailed extent, in the many chains of events, an investigation should proceed, is important, be it an aircraft, ship or railway accident. What is not always clear to the layman is what decides how far back in time? Much depends on the good judgment of the accident investigators. They have the difficult task of not only steering the investigation along the most profitable lines but also in deciding how far down each of the many possible paths of investigation they should go. Too many facts might cloud the proceedings of the formal inquiry. At the same time there are facts and events which could better serve as warnings for the future if they are not included in an Official Report but kept back for the Inspecting Officer's annual report on railway safety.

An example of a chain of events studied at length by the accident investigators is the rear-end collision at Thirsk (Manor House) on the North Eastern in 1892. The signalman at Thirsk fell asleep after accepting a southbound freight and before offering it forward to the next signalbox so that it came to a stand at his home signal. When he awoke, about 13min later, he was confused over the actions he had or thought he had taken, and over the whereabouts of the different trains approaching and leaving his block sections. The signalman to the north of Thirsk offered an up express on the same line as the freight and because of his confusion the Thirsk signalman accepted it, thereby allowing the signalman to his north, who controlled the entrance signals for the up line section, to clear his signals for the express. Unchecked the express raced through the short section and ran into the standing freight train. The inquiry into Thirsk 1892 was able to establish without doubt that the signals and their controls were in order and that the drivers of the trains involved had obeyed their indications. The primary cause was clearly that the signalman at Manor House box had given 'line clear' without verifying that the preceding train had gone forward into the next section. A contributory cause was the failure of the other signalman to question why it took so long before he received 'train out of section' for the freight when he assumed, incorrectly, that it had gone on past Manor House. Another contributory failure was that of the freight train crew who did not bring the Manor House signalman's attention to the fact that they were held at his home signal for an unusual length of time.

In looking at the Thirsk disaster, as a chain of events, we could start at the point in time when the signalman fell asleep, but the chain of tragic events started much earlier. The official inquiry looked closely into the signalman's life before starting his tour of duty so that the causal chain was found to include not just the more important links but the following:

(a) excessively long working hours;
(b) the signalman's child was taken seriously ill on the preceding night;
(c) the signalman spent a worried morning desperately trying to find a doctor;

86

(d) after walking round the countryside he failed to find a doctor and returned home to find his child dead and his wife distraught with grief;

(e) having been without sleep the previous night, fatigued and distressed he tried to get his superiors to find a relief signalman but this they were unable to do and so he found himself back on duty, at night, operating a busy section.

Thirsk 1892 is included just as one example of a series of events which ended in disaster. Following the inquiry and trial for manslaughter, the signalman was acquitted. Another outcome of this accident was a study of the excessive number of hours being worked by railwaymen.

A more recent example of an investigation into a railwayman's off-duty hours is given in the report on the collision between two trains at Copyhold Junction, Southern Region, on 16 December 1972. The Official Report states: '. . . having allowed his (the driver) personal affairs to occupy his thoughts to an extent that he just did not react to a well-sited signal which was showing red . . .'

During his layover time at Brighton the driver concerned had made a long telephone call to a woman friend and this left him no time in which to have a proper, relaxed meal; instead he bought fish and chips to eat in the cab while he drove the train. The inquiry also noted that the driver had recently had an operation because of ulcers. The Copyhold report is an example of the need to look back through a number of apparently unrelated events when looking for the contributory causes of an accident.

At Harrow the primary cause, the failure to obey the indication of a signal, stands at the end of a chain of different and often unrelated events. From all this comes the vital question: why do drivers sometimes pass danger signals? The answer to the question has been sought many times both before and after Harrow. Passing signals at danger has been one of the most frequent causes of railway accidents and one which the investigators have not always been able to explain. If we think about the driver's signal-observing task, particularly in steam days, there is a characteristic which sets it apart from his other duties. It is the way in which a lineside signal is sighted. At first the signal is a long way off and not easily distinguishable from its background. Then it rapidly increases in apparent size. On a straight track, in daylight, with clear air, the signal commands attention from at least a mile off. The position of the semaphore arm can be verified during the minute taken to reach it at, say, 6omph. The multiple-lens colour-light signal, such as the distant for Harrow, stands out even more clearly.

All this is a description of an ideal situation. On the steam railways of Britain, more often than not, an approaching signal appeared not as a steadily growing object but instead as a succession of isolated appearances, as smoke, steam, lineside structures and overbridges came between it and the driver's line of sight. I have already mentioned the conflict between the need for a good forward view and the practice of concentrating the controls on the backhead of the boiler. The best forward view from a large steam locomotive could be had only by craning the neck and head out of the side-window. This meant adopting an awkward posture with the knees hard against the reverser cut-off handle and its gear casing. Some might argue that it did not matter if the driver's controls were awkwardly placed and his position cramped and tiring, for, surely, enginmen were a tough breed? Certainly, they were a hardy lot and, in steam days, tolerated working conditions which in other industries would not have been acceptable. By training and experience the men became part of their machines, and for millions of miles never missed a signal despite the dirt and discomfort of their job. However, was it so essential that their control position should be so poorly designed? The late Dr W. A. Tuplin, an outspoken commentator on steam loco- motive design and operation, ventured, in 1953, before the august body of the Institution of Locomotive Engineers, to criticise the lack of attention to cab design and, in particular, the sometimes inadequate forward view, and the designer's dependence on the driver's acceptance of leaning out of the side-window. The questions which followed his paper and the correspondence it generated did not give me the impression that designers were much concerned. The Harrow report does not say anything about the design or lack of design of loco-motive cabs, either in general, or specifically the cab of *City of Glasgow*. It was as if all concerned had assumed that because for over 100 years enginemen had put up with so many things without protest, then the unfortunate crew of No 46242 were in a familiar situation and one which was common to their work at all times. There was, therefore, no strong reason to look more closely at the design of the locomotive cab.

Returning to the question: why do drivers sometimes pass signals at danger? In 1966 a group of 34 drivers who had passed stop signals was examined and questioned about the circum-stances and possible reasons which caused their failure to see or respond to the signals. It is interesting to note that of the 34 poor eyesight was given as an explanation in only one case; 3 were distracted by anxiety; in 8 cases there was evidence of psychiatric symptoms, and three were special cases. These studies which D. R. Davis made concluded that there were a number of mental processes which could have contributed to the drivers' errors and the following were listed:

panic reaction;
false expectation;
pre-occupation;
distraction;
responding to the wrong signal;
relaxation after stress;
timing errors.

Some of the factors mentioned by D. R. Davis in his study can be related to the Harrow accident, which is also one of the accidents to which he makes specific reference.

False expectation: this can be an important factor in an accident. Yet, to put forward false expectation as a primary cause of Harrow may stretch patience too far when talking about the events between the Perth sleeper restarting from the stop at Watford North Tunnel and the driver apparently not responding to the Harrow distant signal. Could the driver have pressed on to the south, round the curve on the high embankment at Watford, over Bushey water troughs, past Hatch End station and then, with the yellow light of the signal shining through the mist, his 'expectation' turned it to a green light? False expectation can affect all of us at some time or another. There is much evidence about false perception, because of expectation, of colours, shapes, positions of objects and familiar faces. The familiar face situation is one which can be demonstrated when we are waiting for a friend off a crowded train. Every now and then we react to the wrong person in the crowd of people coming toward us. This is because of false expectation and the longer we have to wait the greater the number of false recognitions are made each minute.

The Official Report for an accident at Stobcross on the LMS on 22 February 1939 listed circumstances which included false expectancy and familiarity.

> Its driver felt little or no concern at missing the first signal because, Rule 39 (a) not being applied at Stobcross for up passenger trains to avoid stopping them in the tunnel, he had never found it 'on' at any time during the eleven years he had been travelling over the route.

In Chapter 6 I refer to an accident at Polesworth in 1951 when a driver failed to respond to an 'unexpected' yellow signal.

Preoccupation and Distraction: these are another two possible causes of accidents. The combination of even minor distraction and inattention is a common factor in a number of accidents. One driver, for example, had been troubled by sleepiness and when distracted by other crewmen in the cab had a lapse of 'momentary observation' and overran a signal. A letter to a journal from a driver suggested that a contributory cause of the Harrow accident might have been difficulty with the injector controls which were on the left and under the driver's seat. To get at the control lever and hold it in position to make the injector work, the driver had to reach back and down under the seat. It is possible that the driver of the 46242 had been struggling with this awkwardly placed control just as the yellow distant came into full view for the assumed four seconds.

When talking about preoccupation and distraction it is interesting to note that many studies in different branches of transport have been made of the way in which drivers respond, or fail to respond, to warning signals. The Royal Air Force Institute of Aviation Medicine emphasises that incidents and accidents nearly always happen in circumstances where they are least expected and sometimes the occurrences result from human error due to 'unawareness'. This is a state concerned with preoccupation and distraction but it does not necessarily mean a driver's degree of consciousness. It is concerned with the ways in which he reacts to his surroundings. For example, a sudden change in the usual patterns seen by a driver, such as a signal light coming into his view, may not change his behaviour. He sees the signal but is 'unaware' of it and does not act correctly, if he acts at all, to the signal's meaning. Mistakes which can arise from unawareness can occur in the following situations:

(a) The driver of a train fully appreciates what he sees, but is incapable of taking any action. Although this is a rare situation it can occur, particularly if a driver is so fatigued that he can no longer exert his mental faculties or his muscles.

(b) The driver may clearly see all signals but fails to appreciate their meaning.

(c) A driver sees everything clearly with the exception of one vital signal even though it is fully in his field of view.

(d) A driver may be so preoccupied with his thoughts and his mind wandering to such an extent that he is unaware of the visual scene ahead.

The last condition is rare but even when a driver's attention is suddenly attracted by a noise or bright light, so that he is made aware of his surroundings, it can take some time for him to appreciate fully his circumstances and to take the appropriate control actions. This situation might be allied to the Moorgate tunnel wall collision in 1975. There are two overall reasons why a driver may fail to see or react to a signal. The driver may have too many things to do at once; alternatively, there may be too little to do and in those circumstances a driver can easily be distracted. There is, therefore, an optimum work load which is somewhere between the extreme of inactivity and over activity. If a driver becomes unaware of his surroundings and of the view ahead then something obviously needs to be done to attract his attention. The degree of inattention can range from sleep to panic. In other words a driver is least aware when asleep. He is also least aware when aroused into panic action. A drowsy driver will miss signals and so will an over-excited driver.

There are various ways of controlling to some extent the level of driver attention. One of the most important ways relates to the design of the control position, and this applies just as much to the cab of a locomotive as to the cockpit of an aircraft. A well-designed position with a comfortable, but not too comfortable, seat and an unobstructed view-ahead can help to prevent fatigue which can lead to drowsiness and missed signals. Another way of holding his attention is to give the driver information on how well he is performing his tasks. All this is easier to achieve in the modern locomotive cab than it would have been in the days of steam. In general, a driver's lack of attention or unawareness comes from the amount of work he has to do and the extent to which instruments and signals arouse his attention.

Comments on the subjects of unawareness, attention, and driver behaviour come from general studies of the problems and are not necessarily directly relatable to the steam locomotive driver. One reason for this is that it was not until the steam locomotive was about to be hurried from the British railway scene that research into these subjects was applied to the railway control positions. Therefore, neither the railway nor the investigators concerned with Harrow 1952 had the benefit of our present knowledge about the design of control positions and about human behaviour when fatigued, worried, distracted or mislead by insufficient, incorrect or obscured information.

Did the driver see the distant signal but fail to appreciate its meaning? Possibly, but with an experienced driver unlikely, even though there is evidence for this sort of thing. Furthermore, a yellow signal light is an unambiguous message if seen as 'yellow'. It is not a complicated instruction. There is no 'may be' or 'perhaps'. At Harrow it meant only one thing: 'reduce speed prepared to stop at the outer home signal'. In the extreme, did the driver see all the things he normally expected to see but the one essential part of the picture, the yellow light, escaped his attention? With only four seconds in which to read the signal it is possible that unawareness allowed him to press on to the south oblivious of the danger.

I have already mentioned the danger from over familiarity. This applies to the driving of all types of vehicles, and, as that perceptive writer on the work of the Victorian engine drivers, Michael Reynolds emphasises, this has been a long standing problem:

But in numerous instances, the offence (overshooting and mistaking signals) is committed through the wonderful elasticity of action encouraged by familiarity. Some of the most experienced drivers have come to grief through their habits having become set. Now the sure way to avoid running by signals is to forget that the signal has ever been seen before, and to maintain day after day the same anxiety to sight it as was done in the first instance, or when we first run past it.

Of all the possibilities studied by D. R. Davis, relaxation after stress is very relevant to Harrow, that is provided there had been no mechanical failure. How does the relaxation after stress fit the circumstances of Harrow? If we consider the sequence of events leading up to the collision the stop at Watford Tunnel North box gives a starting point. After the signal stop the driver could have adopted a more relaxed attitude because of the contrast with the fog and dark of the run between Crewe and Watford. The sun was coming up and the fog was less dense and the train in front seemed to have accelerated ahead. Surely, the road was now clear all the way to the terminus at Euston? Associated with this relaxed attitude is 'specific end deterioration', as suggested by Davis, which means 'the worst is over, we are nearly home, stop worrying and relax'. If there was an unexpected and sudden event on the locomotive just north of Headstone Lane and if the crew were in a relaxed frame of mind then having to jerk themselves suddenly into a state of action could have produced a few seconds of confusion, to which would be added their annoyance that something should have gone wrong just when they were all set to finish the journey. The distant signal goes by unseen.

As well as thinking about the reasons why drivers pass signals when they should not it is important also to examine the signals themselves. They, too, exhibit the human characteristics of failing to be seen, or, if seen, are misunderstood. How do you give a signal so that its message is emphatic and clear? Once again we are back to AWS and all the other devices which have been and still are used to attract a driver's attention and to act should he fail to see or respond to the signal's information.

5

The trains and their equipment

Before looking at some of the more technical aspects of the accident, particularly the braking system, couplings, tail-markers and the use of gas in the kitchen car, a detailed description is needed of the three trains.

First, the 'innocent party', the Tring–London local. The 07.31 out of Tring southbound was hauled by tank-engine No 42389, a 2-6-4 weighing just over 86 tons. This two-cylinder locomotive had been built at Derby in 1934 to a design prepared by the staff of Sir Henry Fowler. These 2-6-4s, both parallel and taper boiler versions, were the mainstay of inner and outer suburban services. Their crews achieved good point-to-point timings by accelerating vigorously from each stop. I have mentioned already that No 42389 was running bunker first, as was usual when hauling up trains; that is, those going inwards to the terminus at Euston.

The local consisted of nine coaches, two more than the usual seven coaches on the Euston–Watford–Bletchley outer suburban services because extensive track and signalling works at Euston that autumn had made it necessary to cancel the following train and the extra coaches were intended to ease overcrowding on the 07.31. About 800 passengers were packed into the 74 compartments, an average of 11 people to each. The coaches of the local were traditional British suburban stock of the period with side doors, knee-to-knee cross-bench seats each

95

ostensibly seating six, giving 12 seats to a compartment if everyone squeezed up; there was no through corridor or gang-way between coaches. Those passengers at Harrow who could not find a vacant seat had to stand hard against the bony knees of their more fortunate seated companions. The local was third class only. Ironically the two oldest coaches were at the rear and therefore the first to be savaged by the Pacific of the up express. They, the eighth and ninth vehicles, had been built by the Midland Railway in 1921 and 1916 respectively and had all-timber bodies. The last had timber headstocks, and pas-sengers had little protection from even a minor accident let alone protection from a 500 ton express overtaking at 50mph or more. The other seven coaches included two other all-timber bodied types of 1928 vintage marshalled in the fifth and sixth positions and with the steel-panelled, timber-framed brake third No 21183 as the seventh vehicle with its brake-compart-ment to the rear; on most of the outer-suburban workings on this line it would have been the last coach of the train. All the vehicles had steel underframes but the first four coaches, like the seventh, were of composite body construction with timber body frames, consisting of upright and longitudinal wooden members, with wooden partitions to form the compartments. The framework, including the roof, was covered by 16 gauge steel panels and therefore slightly more resistant to collapse in an accident than an all-wood body. However, as the photo-graphs on page 53 clearly show, the brake third had its steel panels, along with the body framework swept completely away from the underframe floor. This coach had entered service only that year, so that even as late as 1952 'modern' suburban coach-building practice in Britain still relied on timber rather than all-steel construction. This must have been an acceptable practice because no one in authority appears to have questioned it on the grounds of safety.

The three locomotives involved in the double collision, dis-counting the engine of the local which was undamaged, were severely knocked about, so much so that two were eventually scrapped. The engine of the up express was Stanier Pacific No 46242, *City of Glasgow* of power classification 8P. It was built at Crewe in 1940 as a streamlined Coronation type and finished in LMS maroon with golden-yellow 'speed' lines along the sides. In later years the bulbous nose and smooth casing were removed and it re-emerged from Crewe works as a conventionally attired Pacific with side running boards and smoke deflectors. The loaded weight of the *City of Glasgow* was nominally 161 tons 12 cwt. The four 16½in diameter, 28in stroke cylinders were supplied with steam from a tapered boiler of 6ft 5½in maximum diameter with a Belpaire firebox having a grate area of 50sq ft. The maximum working pressure was 250psi. It was altogether a big locomotive which, when in good condition, was capable of hauling 500 ton trains effortlessly up and down the long main line with its many gradients and twists through the Midland counties, through Cumbria and the lowlands of Scotland.

After the accident the *City of Glasgow* was re-railed and pulled clear of the station and subjected to a minute examination to make sure that no part, however small, had failed, thereby distracting the crew so that they missed seeing the distant signal. As the Official Report records, nothing untoward was found other than a broken-off water-gauge drain-cock which was assumed to have been broken by the front of the tender when it drove hard against the boiler backplate. But, as I have mentioned in Chapter 4, this was disputed. Eventually the battered *City of Glasgow* was given an extensive overhaul, with much of the front-end replaced, before returning to service so that once again it worked on West Coast route expresses. It remained on top-link work until 1963 when it gave way to the more efficient but far less romantic diesels and, later, electric locomotives, whose pantographs now hiss under the 400 miles of 25,000 volt contact wires which stretch from London to Glasgow.

The 20.15 Perth–London sleeper consisted of eleven coaches, the oldest built in 1925 and the newest in 1950. Coupled next to the locomotive was a Western Region all-wood milk van, followed by a wooden-bodied brake van built in 1925. Then came a corridor third which, like the remaining coaches of the train, had timber framing covered with 16-gauge steel panels. The fourth and fifth coaches were respectively a brake third and a first and third class composite. These five leading vehicles finished up as so much scrap at the bottom of the heap of wreckage, with their steel panelling torn off or crumpled as if it were paper. The sixth coach of the Perth train, a 1933 corridor third finished up virtually intact, as did the following five coaches which were pulled clear of the wreck soon after the accident to make way for the breakdown cranes. The last five coaches were four sleeping cars and a brake van and their occupants were shaken but not injured by the violent end to the long night journey. The numbers of dead and injured might have been far larger had the train been full; as it happened, only about 85 people were on board.

The 08.00 out of Euston for Liverpool and Manchester was made up of 15 coaches hauled by two locomotives and altogether weighed 737 tons. The eight leading coaches bore the brunt of the impact; the other seven were little damaged and apart from having to re-rail the front bogie of the ninth coach it was possible to pull them clear of the wreckage to give the cranes room to work. Like the up express, the Liverpool train's coaches had steel-panelled bodies on timber framework mounted on steel underframes. There were, however, three important exceptions, for the fourth, sixth and eleventh coaches were new British Railways standard designs of all-steel construction. The ends of these new coaches were reinforced and equipped with automatic centre-couplers and Pullman type gangways. These three withstood the effects of the collision well and even the fourth, which finished up on the station platform to the right of the sixth coach of the Perth train, kept its four passenger compartments intact though it lost its brake van section as it was hurled up under the footbridge and over the top of the other two trains before crashing down on to the platform, close to where the guard of the local train was sheltering from the effects of the first collision. The second all-steel standard coach, marshalled sixth in the Liverpool train, ended up on top of *City of Glasgow* but, despite the fearful battering suffered by its ends, the body kept its shape. In 1952 the building programme for new passenger stock with all-steel bodies, automatic centre-couplers and Pullman gangways was only just getting under way and there were few complete sets of these new and stronger coaches. The effectiveness of the Buckeye couplers was thus not put to the test in the accident because they were not in use and were swung down out of the way so that the new coaches could be joined to the older stock using the screw-link couplings and side buffers.

The eighth coach was a kitchen car and although it was newly painted in the standard 'red and cream' livery of the period it was an example of 'mutton dressed as lamb'. A close inspection of the builder's plate revealed the date 1926. An even closer look, underneath the frames, revealed the compressed gas cylinders which supplied the cooking ranges, and lighting, of which more later. In all, the London–Liverpool train was a typical London Midland Region train of its time, a mixed bag of coach designs and ages which, while of great interest to the coach historian, did not represent the best of British practice.

The Liverpool express was hauled by a 4-6-0 No 45637, *Windward Isles*, of Stanier's Jubilee class, power classification 6P, as pilot engine, and the train engine was No 46202, a 4-6-2, power classification 8P, named *Princess Anne*. *Windward Isles* had three cylinders, a taper boiler and a narrow Belpaire type firebox, and with its tender weighed, in working order, 133 tons. The photograph on page 71 shows the tremendous damage it suffered from its head-on collision with the derailed *City of Glasgow*. All but the more massive parts have been smashed off

99

or buckled up. During the time when it hit the wreckage of the first collision, glanced off the unyielding front of the Pacific, hurtled across the platform to the left, slid on to its side and came to rest across the electric lines on the west side of the station, the three cylinder castings were smashed, the bogie broken into pieces and scattered and the front frames were folded back as far as the first coupled axle. The less substantial running plates and the cab were torn away. No wonder the last run of No 45637 was to the scrap heap.

The train engine, *Princess Anne*, had an interesting history even before the events of 1952, for it started life in 1935 unofficially known as the *Turbomotive*. This was basically a Stanier Princess class Pacific with a steam turbine in place of the conventional four-cylinder reciprocating propulsion of the other LMS Pacifics. After running nearly half a million miles with varying degrees of reliability, including taking its turn with heavy wartime loads, it was decided, early in 1952, that it was no longer practicable to keep it in service as an isolated example, particularly as the main turbine was worn out. Thus it re-emerged from Crewe works as a four-cylinder Pacific, a hybrid with features of both Princess and Coronation types, now carrying the name *Princess Anne* but retaining its BR number. The photograph on page 17 shows No 46202 lying on its side, where it had followed the pilot engine across the platform and down on to the electric lines. Although not so badly damaged as *Windward Isles*, the decision was taken to scrap her. The boiler was not too badly damaged and it was put on the spare list for use by other Princess Pacifics needing a boiler renewal. The withdrawal of No 46202 was a factor in gaining authority to build the solitary three-cylinder BR standard Pacific *Duke of Gloucester*.

One thing which distinguishes the railway from other forms of transport is the low rolling resistance of the steel wheel on steel rail. This has been the key factor in the haulage of heavy loads and needing horse power much less than with other forms of land transport. Unfortunately, if the resistance to motion is low then the ability to stop quickly is also low. It is possible for a pneumatic-tyred road vehicle to stop, *in ideal conditions,* from 60mph within about 100ft, whereas a train at that speed needs nearly half a mile in which to pull up. The braking system can be fierce enough to lock the wheels but however effective this is, the thing that really matters is the adhesion, or grip between wheel and rail. If the brakes lock the wheels and they start to slide, the brakes have to be released and reapplied. It takes some seconds before the effects of a brake application are sensed by the driver, with variations depending on gradient, weather conditions, the state of the rail and the type of train. At Harrow the driver of the up Perth express appears to have made a full brake application at about the time when the up fast outer home signal came into sight. There was no time for a carefully controlled stop; it was all or nothing.

Braking is essentially a means of changing energy from one form to another. A moving train has energy, that is kinetic energy, which is proportional to its weight and to the square of the speed. The Perth–London express at 55mph had over 50,000ft/ton of this energy. What happened to the 50,000ft/ton of energy between the instant when the train was moving at 55mph and when it finally came to rest with the locomotive buried in the wreckage of the local train? The energy was partly converted into heat from the friction of the brake blocks binding on the wheel tyres but much of it was spent in destroying, by pushing, bending and smashing up, the coaches of the local train as well as parts of the station.

The Official Report, paragraph 44, records that Guard Kent said that the train was moving at 50–5mph when there was a severe brake application and he saw the vacuum gauge in his brake van go almost instantly to zero. This was followed about five seconds later by three violent forward lurches and then by an equally violent rebound. A ticket-collector gave evidence that the brakes went hard on just before the collision and a sleeping-car attendant suggested that it was only two seconds before the crash from the time he felt the brakes going on. It is not difficult to reconstruct the probable chain of events by working back from the collision point, but this is somewhat of an academic exercise because no one knows for certain how the driver reacted to the sudden appearance of unexpected circumstances. In the 200yd, or less, visibility and looking into the sun, he may have seen a signal or the buildings on the approach to Harrow and his brain would have instantly registered both a question and a sense of danger. But it would have taken at least two seconds before his brain signalled the muscles to operate the controls and in particular to move the brake application lever fully over to the left, the position in which the handle was found after the accident. Even when the brake handle had been set to the full-on position there still remained seconds needed for the brakes to take full effect and before the witnesses on the train could have felt the train slowing down.

Therefore, it might have been only ten seconds away from the collision that the driver realised where he was and saw the danger signals. In those ten seconds the train moved about 800ft which, when retraced back along the line, brings us to Harrow up fast inner home signal. From the point at which the inquiry assumed the brakes had been fully applied to the point at which the Pacific finally stopped leaping and ploughing among the coaches of the local train, the express moved over 400ft. This means that, and using an average speed of half the initial 55mph over the distance, the locomotive was hitting everything in its path with enough energy to toss a double-deck London bus 1,700ft into the air. But all this is an approximation because the reduction of speed from the first contact with the standing train to coming to a rest was accomplished in a series of jerks as, successively, different parts of the local were scattered or destroyed.

Despite the existence of a national railway system, each

region retained in 1952 some of its pre-nationalisation and even pre-grouping practices and equipment. This applied particularly to the methods used for braking trains. The railways in Britain either used the Westinghouse or the vacuum brake depending on origins in pre-grouping times. The former is also usually referred to as the 'air' brake and the latter as the 'vacuum', even though this is also an 'air' brake because atmospheric pressure is used to apply the brakes. The Westinghouse is a compressed air brake system working at pressures greater than one atmosphere (15psi approximately). Compressed air, in the train pipe connecting all vehicles and their brake components, is used to control the release and admission of air at the brake cylinders as well as supplying the air at pressure to the individual reservoirs of each coach or wagon. The vacuum brake, working at pressures less than atmospheric, also uses a train pipe for control but instead of supplying air at pressure to each vehicle it is used to exhaust the system to the required level of vacuum. Control is excercised by varying the degree of vacuum in the train pipe thereby operating the valves which control the admission of air at each brake cylinder.

Both the Westinghouse and the vacuum are termed automatic because the brakes will be applied if the pressure in the train pipe changes because of a leak. The leak can be accidental such as when a hose parts between two coaches, or deliberate and controlled when the driver opens the brake valve on the locomotive, which, in effect, is a controllable 'leak'. With both systems of braking a parted train will come to a standstill as the ruptured hoses open the train pipe to atmospheric pressure, a small technical fact sometimes conveniently ignored by writers of fiction. However, with both methods of braking, trains have run away but only because the system has not been checked before starting and was subsequently found to be not fully operative. For example, if one of the shut-off cocks at the ends of each vehicle fitted with the compressed air brake is closed and none of the trainmen notices it because the brake continuity test has not been carried out, then, although the system appears to be functioning, all that part of the train behind the closed cock will be isolated and the brakes out of use.

A brief history of brakes on British trains may help to show why the London Midland Region used steam brakes on locomotives and vacuum brakes on passenger trains. During the first 40 years of railway development there were many accidents which might have been avoided had the trains been fitted with efficient brakes. The years 1862/3/4 were particularly bad ones for accidents which might have been prevented or their consequences made less severe had there been continuous brakes. The railways in those years came in for much criticism in the press, so much so that the Queen intervened by commanding her personal secretary to convey to the board of every railway with an office in London 'Her Majesty's deepest misgivings on the subject'. It was not until the Royal Commission of 1874 that regulations were proposed relating to the provision of effective brakes. At that time the majority of trains relied for both service and emergency stopping on hand brakes applied by the guards and brakesmen stationed at intervals along a train. In an emergency a driver might assist the handbrakesmen by reversing his engine.

Of all the Victorian railways, the Midland was one of the most responsive to safety and for a time considered seriously adopting the Westinghouse air brake for passenger stock to comply with the persistent prodding by the Board of Trade about fitting reliable and effective continuous brakes. In 1869 the Midland tried the Wilkin and Clarke chain brake but it was not suitable or reliable, particularly in winter conditions. When James Allport, the Midland's energetic general manager, returned from an 1872 tour of North American railroads he recommended that the Westinghouse system be tried and a number of locomotives and coach sets were equipped, including the two Midland Pullman cars of that period. By 1875, the year of the Newark brake trials, the Midland's Westinghouse equipment had been made fully automatic, that is, the brakes would be applied automatically to all parts of a train should a coupling or brake hose part. At the Newark trials a Midland train of 203 tons running at 52mph was braked to a stop in 19 seconds and 913ft and it seemed for a time that George Westinghouse's vigorous sales campaign in Britain would gain the crowning success of 'capturing' the Midland. But it was not to be for, despite the advantages of the Westinghouse, a combination of minor faults and arguments over payments soured relationships between the two companies. In the end the Midland adopted the Sanders vacuum brake and by 1879 it was an all vacuum line.

Within three years of Newark a Royal Commission was given the authority of the Railway Returns (Continuous Brakes) Act 1878 which made the fitting of continuous (not then automatic) brakes compulsory on passenger trains. Of course, as was customary, the Act did not specify any particular type or manufacturer of brake. With the Regulation of Railways Act 1889 came the automatic brake requirement for passenger trains. Although the railways had adopted the continuous brake without too much protest they were reluctant to add an automatic feature to their simple non-automatic systems. It was argued that there was a greater risk of failure from a more elaborate system and that the brake might automatically apply itself when no emergency stop was intended, or might fail to operate when needed altogether. However, with train weights and speeds increasing year by year the 1889 Act was eventually fully implemented and the automatic continuous brake was fitted to all passenger stock on all railways. Which make of brake? This question had to be answered by each company's engineer in the light of his own experience and type of traffic.

There were companies which favoured the Westinghouse and others who preferred the vacuum. As we have seen, the Midland settled eventually for the vacuum, as did the LNWR and the Lancashire & Yorkshire. When the LMS emerged from the 1923 grouping it adopted the vacuum as its standard system because three of its major constituents were vacuum lines. Of the other companies which formed the LMS, the Caledonian and the London, Tilbury & Southend (absorbed by the Midland in 1912) retained the Westinghouse for those trains which normally kept within those systems. It is interesting to note that the two companies of pre-grouping days which operated the fastest regular trains, the Caledonian and the North Eastern, used the Westinghouse brake. This suggests that its speed of response, power, and quick release, compared with the vacuum, had something to do with the elan with which their drivers controlled the fast trains. The weight of fact which influenced the LMS toward the vacuum brake, which it passed on to the LM Region, is set out in the table Appendix II.

As we have seen, some of the coaches of the London–Liverpool train were British Railways standard designs fitted with automatic centre-couplers based on North American practice. The automatic centre-coupler is the alternative to the standard British and European screw-link and side buffer type of connection between coaches which had been used extensively since the middle of the last century. The automatic coupler was introduced to Britain, along with Pullman cars, from the USA and during the last decade of the nineteenth century the Great Northern started to fit all new express stock with this type of coupler; the North Eastern also used it for coaches, which were part of the East Coast Joint Stock fleet, and it was used on new coach sets for the Great Central's 1899 London extension services. Of the railways of the 1923 grouping, the GWR and the LMS did not use automatic couplers other than for a few special sets, notably the later vehicles of the LMS royal train, whereas, both the LNER, from its GNR and NER inheritance, and the Southern steadily fitted all locomotive-hauled main line coaches with automatic couplers during the 1930s.

The automatic centre-coupler is today a familiar feature

along with wide Pullman-type gangways and retractable buffers at the ends of British Railways coaches, but in 1952, on the LMR, this type of connection between vehicles was very much in the minority. Apart from reducing the gap between coaches and simplifying the gangway connection, the automatic centre-coupler is designed to prevent telescoping during an accident by holding the ends of coaches firmly together so that they will not ride up or push under the frame of the next, as happened to some of the screw-link coupled coaches at Harrow. The development of the automatic centre-coupler in the USA in the 1880s was encouraged not so much by the need to prevent telescoping but by the urgent need to reduce the number of deaths and serious injuries to railmen who had to go between cars to drop home the awkward pin of the link-and-pin couplers then common, while cars were being shunted together.

In the collision at Castlecary 1937 on the Edinburgh–Glasgow line of the LNER, the automatic couplers and Pullman gangways proved their worth. According to the Official Report: 'The retention of alignment of the Edinburgh express in the rear of the third coach was remarkable. If the tender had been fitted with this coupler the extraordinary overriding of the first three coaches might have been prevented.' Castlecary was an accident in which there were a number of factors similar to those of Harrow, particularly as a standing train was hit at speed by another hauled by a heavy Pacific locomotive. The Inspecting Officer, Colonel Mount, determined from calculations that the momentum of the express as it hit the tail of the standing train was no less than 54,000ft/tons. The speed just before the brakes were applied was about 70mph, 15mph faster than at Harrow. When the Pacific *Grand Parade* crashed into the rear of the Dundee train it proceeded to crush and splinter the coaches into a mass of twisted steel frames and shattered woodwork over about the same length as did *City of Glasgow* at Harrow.

Another accident which demonstrated the effectiveness of

the automatic couplers in preventing telescoping was the collision at Welwyn Garden City on 15 June 1935. The low death roll, only 14 out of 300 passengers in the two trains, emphasised the resistance of the automatic centre-couplers. The last but one coach in the train, which was hit by the overtaking express, was of all-steel construction and although both its bogies were swept away it remained coupled and supported by the coach in front so that there were no serious injuries to the passengers. The colliding train, hauled by a K3 class 2-6-0 travelling at about 60mph, had the first three coaches joined by automatic centre-couplers and these held firmly together and prevented telescoping, although the first was partly telescoped against the tender because this had a screw-link coupling. Coaches four to nine, with screw-links, had severely damaged ends.

A 15mph head-on collision between two trains outside Hull Paragon on 14 February 1927 resulted in the deaths of 12 passengers in the telescoped coaches. Both trains after the accident were still nearly in line and the two locomotives stood face-to-face, damaged but repairable, but the steel underframed, wooden-bodied coaches had telescoped one into another for nearly half the length of each. As so often happened, the screw-link couplings between the coaches gave way, allowing the steel frames to slice into the wooden coach bodies and their occupants.

Would the use of all-steel coaches for the local train have reduced the number of casualties at Harrow? The Official Report makes the point that the wreckage might have been less compact and the number killed and injured less if a greater proportion of the rolling stock had been of the latest all-steel type and rigidly coupled. The engine of the southbound express struck the last coach of the standing local at a point in line with the top of the platform ramp, and telescoped the last three vehicles into the length of one. The wooden bodies were swept away by the Pacific and by the telescoping action as the underframe of the last coach rode over the frame of the next and then under the seventh which, although of more advanced construction, with steel panelling, nevertheless had its body crumpled up and forced under the footbridge. The underframes of the last three coaches were then tossed aside by the colliding locomotive and finished up in a tangled heap of metal on the platform. Their bogies were driven into a heap beneath the main wreckage.

Eighteen years before Harrow, after the Winwick rear-end collision of 1934, the then President of the LMS, Sir Josiah Stamp, was quoted in a newspaper: 'I have heard it suggested that all-steel coaches would save life in railway disasters, but this is a matter on which there is a wide difference of opinion. At any rate it is safe to say that the rolling stock had nothing to do with this particular accident. Both the carriages in which the loss of life took place were of the usual modern type, with steel undercarriages and wooden bodies.' To imply that in 1934 'modern' type meant steel underframes with wooden bodies suggests that the LMS had still a long way to go towards ensuring the safety of passengers or, the chairman was poorly briefed by his public relations department. Possibly, the truth of the matter is that, at that time, none of the railway companies was willing to abandon traditional methods of coach building and embark on all-steel construction because it would have meant an extensive re-organisation of their workshops, and because timber was cheaper than steel.

If, as the Official Report suggests, the coaches of the local train at Harrow had been of all-steel construction and rigidly joined by automatic centre-couplers how might they have resisted better the mighty blow struck them by *City of Glasgow?*

Many factors in this type of accident must be taken into account and for most we can only make a guess at their effect or consequence. We can reconstruct the accident using coaches of all-steel type with automatic centre-couplers, the bodies of the coaches and their underframes forming a rigid, welded whole. With this type of rolling stock it is possible that the local train would have been driven bodily forward for some distance until the sideways resistance of the centre-couplers relaxed and allowed each coach to turn to cross the track followed by some of the couplers tearing out of their mountings. The coaches might then have finished up side-by-side. But other factors might have altered this hypothetical sequence of events. For example, the local train was alongside a stone platform, and only 11ft to its right was another platform. These two structures might have prevented the familiar zig-zag wreck pattern and made some of the coaches ride up and over the platforms. The zig-zag is often a feature of accidents involving rigidly coupled stock when a train is able to spread itself to both sides of the track, but in the confines of a station, such as at Harrow, this is less likely. Had the local train and the colliding train coaches zig-zagged in the middle of the station then the wreckage would have presented a different form of barrier to the London–Liverpool train which then would have driven at about 60mph into a coach standing nearly at an angle to its track and the whole pattern of the accident might then have been very different.

In general all-steel rigidly-coupled coaches are better able to resist the effects of derailments and end-on collisions, provided the couplers are not damaged. At Winsford on 26 December 1962, a rear-end collision resulted in the last coach of a standing train telescoping into the next for half its length despite the use of automatic centre-couplers. As in some other similar collisions, the couplers were fractured or torn out of their seating so allowing the coaches to over-ride each other. At Harrow rigid couplings might have lessened the effects, provided the forces involved were not so great as to fracture or force the jaws of the couplers open.

The history of the tail marker on the railways of Britain is easy to write about because there has been really only one basic type used from the dawn of the steam railway, into the twentieth century and still used even now with diesel and electric traction. This is the oil lamp with a red lens. It serves two purposes, first as a warning light or 'light-house' protecting the tail of a train, and second, it indicates the last vehicle of a train so that signalmen along the line can verify that each train is complete, which, in the days of loose-coupled, unbraked freight trains was very important.

In those parts of the world where the signalling system is either rudimentary or even non-existent and much of the responsibility for avoiding a tail-end collision devolves on the train driver, adequate marking and illumination of the end of the last vehicle of a train is very important. Even on signalled routes in some countries high intensity tail marker lights are used; in contrast, in Britain the operating rules and the signalling system are meant to perform the primary function of preventing collisions. Those occasions when a driver might find himself bearing down on another train at speed are assumed to be rare. In steam days if a driver missed the feeble oil lamp of a signal then he was just as likely to miss the feeble oil lamp guarding the tail of the train in front.

From time to time railway companies tried to improve the visibility of trains by using colours and patterns but, in general, the last vehicle of a British train presented and still presents only a dark shape against the often murky background, with only the feeble glimmer of one red oil lamp to distinguish it from the track and lineside structures. The LBSCR, LSWR, LTSR and the NLR painted the ends of some coaches and brake-vans a bright red or vermilion in order to make them more conspicuous and today multiple-unit diesel and electric trains have yellow ends. The effectiveness of these colours as attention-getters diminished with weathering and an accumulation of grime. Electric tail lights are now provided on some but by no means all trains.

In general, it cannot be recorded that the railways of Britain worried overmuch about the conspicuity of the tail-end of a train; for that matter neither did they do much about the front end, although these comments refer primarily to steam railways; in recent years more thought has been given to this subject.

Possibly the attitude to conspicuity on the part of the steam railways was partly based on the answer to the question: 'Why add a belt to the braces when we have developed operating practices and signalling systems intended to prevent collisions?'. All the same, there were a number of occasions when either the system or the man failed and a train stood on the line with nothing protecting it from another except the vigilance of the driver of the oncoming train and the conspicuity of the end coach.

In retrospect we can visualise the scene at Harrow with the sun shining through the mist, the high red oil lights and red arms of the home signals and the grey end of the local train merging into the diffused background as the Perth–London train approached unchecked until the last moment. It is doubtful that the driver saw the local until it was far too late. Most likely he became aware that something was dreadfully wrong when the outer home signal came into his view. Then, within a second or two, he saw the arm of the inner home for the oil light would have hardly been visible in the misty daylight; he might even have concentrated for a moment on the brighter electric light of the starting signal, which was green for the local to proceed and, moreover, was at eye level. Once he realised what was about to happen he must have made every attempt possible to stop his heavy train in the shortest distance.

No amount of bright paint, dramatic patterning and tail lights could have saved the local. However, there is always a doubt and I feel that, with the easily acquired clarity of hindsight, all trains in those days needed at least two bright, red lights and distinctive pattern of contrasting colours at the end, to break through the sometimes enveloping clouds of steam and smoke, mist and the dark of night. Even today rear-end marking could be improved on many trains.

Despite the history of the terrible consequences from using compressed gas for lighting and cooking in trains the kitchen-car of the London–Liverpool train used gas. Fortunately, the damage to the car released all the gas in one go. Had it escaped slowly through damaged fittings it might have fed a great fire amid the wreckage. The use of gas, as an alternative and eventual replacement for the rape-oil lamps of mid Victorian years, originated with Julius Pintsch of Prussia, and his system of lighting was first used in Britain on the Metropolitan in 1876. Until the advent of electric lighting—and the first experiments in electric lights were in the late 1880s—Pintsch gas was the usual method of illuminating passenger compartments and, incidentally, contributed much to the characteristic smell of a British train. The conversion to electricity from gas was slow and even after World War II gas-lit coaches were still running. This was fifty years after the Midland Railway accidents at Wellingborough 1898, Cudworth 1905, Hawes Junction 1910 and Ais Gill 1913, the effects of which had been made worse by the bursting of the compressed-gas cylinders and the ignition of escaping gas. These accidents involving fire occurred on a railway which was often in the van of technical progress and although the Midland experimented with electric lighting, the decision was taken in 1884 by the Traffic Committee, to fit main-line stock with compressed oil-gas. As E. G. Barnes succinctly comments: 'In this one short and simple resolution lay the death sentences for the victims of the Hawes Junction and the Ais Gill disasters then a quarter of a century distant'. Yet in the 1930s the LMS was building *new* kitchen and restaurant cars, with gas for cooking, *and* lighting in some cases.

6

Automatic warning and braking

The conclusions of the official inquiry into Harrow 1952 included, as the principal cause, the failure of the driver to respond to the yellow signal but went on to urge the adoption of an automatic warning system (AWS).

In *The Engineer* 10 July 1953 an editorial highlighted the relationship between the accident and AWS:

> Major disasters on the British railways by their very rarity never fail to arouse feelings of particular horror, and for some little time afterwards the burden of many letters in the national and in the technical press is to seek means whereby 'it could never happen again'. Sometimes, as in the case of the Armagh runaway collision in 1889, the public conscience has been so deeply stirred as to secure the adoption of increased safety measures by Act of Parliament, but those who have studied the report of the Government inspecting officers over the past forty-five years cannot fail to have noticed the frequency with which some form of automatic train control has been recommended. In retrospect, these officers appear to have been little more than voices crying in the wilderness. But now the catastrophe of Harrow last autumn appears to have done for ATC what Armagh did for continuous brakes and for the absolute block system; and the British Transport Commission is now prepared to consider financial authority for a scheme that will eventually cost some £17 million.

Until the general adoption of means whereby a driver is given an audible or additional in-the-cab visual indication of 'stop', 'approach with caution' and 'proceed', or a target speed indication, lineside signals have been the universally accepted method of protecting trains. Drivers came before signals. Until the introduction of fixed location lineside signals, from about 1850 onwards, the driver of a train was entrusted with its safe conduct with little intervention of others. A driver, in those days, set out on a journey in circumstances analogous to those of the captain of a ship in uncharted waters. It was his responsibility and his alone to watch out for hazards and above all to avoid crashing into another train. He was sometimes advised by policemen by hand or flag signals if another train had passed a given point a few minutes in front of him but that did not guarantee that the train ahead was continuing at the same interval or at all. With the further development of the steam railway, lineside signals eventually replaced the policemen who provided the first 'mechanical' method for preventing collisions. Signals were put in on the busier sections of the railways but for many years they were still largely advisory rather than mandatory in intent.

Railway signalling is a story in itself but one aspect is pertinent to this book, the relationship between a driver's actions and the indications of the lineside signals. On all railways there were and still are operating rules and the most important of these, in the style of a commandment, is: 'thou shalt not disregard the indications of the signals'. Lineside signals were, until alternative systems were developed from about 1900 onward, the method by which those ordering the running of trains could communicate unambiguously with drivers of trains. I use the word unambiguously deliberately because the other methods of communication, such as the written order, shouting, waving arms and lanterns, can be misinterpreted. A lineside signal with, say, two indications, precisely differentiated, Danger and Clear, gives a precise message to the driver without the nuances and potential errors of alternative methods. Provided the signals are obeyed, safety from collisions and derailments or from running through adversely set points, is achieved but whenever there is a human element, as a link in the chain of vital operations, there is the possibility of failure. Human failings, unlike mechanical or electrical breakdowns, cannot be predicted. In an attempt to improve the link between the signals and drivers hundreds of ideas have been patented, ranging from the simple to the complex. Equipment and systems have been proposed and sometimes developed and put into use, for raising the standards of railway safety by ensuring that signal indications are both seen or heard and acted upon.

In North America, the many ideas tried included placing the semaphore signals close against the side of the track with the arm pointing across the track, instead of, as is more usual, pointing away from the track to which it refers. If a driver ignored the stop indication of this type of signal, the locomotive would hit the semaphore arm and smash it; the resulting noise and shock conveyed forcibly to the driver the fact that he had overrun the signal, and, presumably, there was the added shock of knowing he would have to pay for a new signal. In an endeavour to bring the signal 'into the cab' a number of ideas were tried from the middle of the 19th century onwards. In addition to the technical problems which had to be overcome, there was the fundamental difference of opinion among railway officers over the degree of authority to be exercised by any form of cab signalling, train control or warning system. For example, should a system just advise the driver, or should the device automatically apply the brakes? Essentially it was a matter of how much control should be given to the driver. Another aspect of cab signalling and automatic warning and stop system design is the variation in operating conditions among the different railways. It is one thing to design equipment which will automatically bring London underground trains to a stop on passing at a red signal, when all trains are in standard formations and speed rarely exceeds 40mph, but another matter when, as in North America, for example, six or more locomotives might be pulling and pushing a mile-long train. It is also another matter when, as in Britain, trains varied in both speed and weight, from an engine with one coach to a 500-ton passenger train running at 80mph. Each type of train and operating conditions, such as the method of signalling, signal spacing and type of brake, required a particular safety system and it was not easy to devise a mechanical cab signalling device which would suit all these variations.

The Official Report for Harrow devoted nearly 5 of its 37 pages to the subject of automatic train control (ATC), today known as the automatic warning system (AWS). What is AWS? It is a system which automatically and without the intervention of the driver warns him of an adverse signal and, if he fails to reduce speed, automatically applies the brakes. AWS was evolved from the Great Western Railway's ATC but unlike the latter's title does what it says: it automatically warns, whereas GWR automatic train control ATC was a slightly misleading description because the system did not really control trains other than to apply the brakes. Not unexpectedly, the Harrow Official Report gave credit to the GWR for the example it had set with its extensive ATC installation. The first section of the GWR to be equipped was the Twyford to Henley branch in January 1906 and was followed by a programme to equip all the major routes with ATC, so that by November 1939 the GWR had 2852 miles of track and 3250 locomotives operated within the protection of ATC. Altogether there were 2114 contact ramps. The result, GWR drivers were generally able to run on time despite fog; the reassuring short ring of the ATC bell indicated that the distant signal they were about to pass was clear or the horn sounding meant it was at caution. Either way the driver had audible indication of the signal location. On other railways in a 'peasoup' fog drivers had to grope their way from signal to signal, and on occasions they had to send their fireman up a signal post ladder to check the position of the semaphore arm.

The GWR cab signalling system was not the only one used in

Britain. Both the North Eastern and the Great Central railways tried cab signalling and train-stop systems. Unfortunately they were installed at a time when the after effects of World War I and the pending grouping of Britain's railway companies were not favourable to isolated systems. The GWR and its ATC entered the grouping era hardly changed whereas the NER and the GCR were merged with other companies and with different operating practices and equipment, and different ideas about cab signalling. The history of the NER cab signalling equipment started in January 1876 when John Hardy of the Cliff House Iron Works, West Hartlepool, submitted to the locomotive superintendent of the NER, Edward Fletcher, a method of informing drivers of the aspect of a distant signal which might be obscured by fog or snow. Hardy's apparatus consisted of a trip-lever fitted to the front of a locomotive which was linked to the engine's whistle control. If the distant signal was at caution then the ramp, linked to the signal operating rod, was raised. As the locomotive moved over the raised ramp the trip-lever was lifted, thereby sounding the whistle.

Like many other good schemes, Hardy's warning system was as simple as possible; however, it was not adopted and, perhaps, it came too soon in the history of railway technology to be appreciated.

Cab signalling on the NER was revived in 1894 when W. L Raven, later Sir Vincent Raven, and C. Baister proposed a system which was similar to that devised by Hardy. The Raven-Baister equipment was first tested on the Darlington–Barnard Castle line at a distant signal on the approach to the delightfully named Merrybent Junction. Patented in December 1895, this new NER system used rail-mounted trip-levers, similar to those used eventually on the London underground. When a distant signal was at caution the trip-arm was raised so as to strike a corresponding lever below the locomotive. This pushed up a vertical rod connected to the whistle valve. Unlike the earlier Hardy system, the Raven-Baister apparatus used a special warning whistle and not the normal locomotive whistle to indicate an adverse distant signal. Another important feature and one which anticipated the later British AWS, the apparatus had to be re-set or cancelled by the driver, otherwise the warning whistle would continue to sound. With the Hardy equipment the whistle sounded only during the few seconds the locomotive was passing over the ramp.

Between 1896 and 1901, the NER equipped 237 signals with cab signalling track units, which by that time was being called the Fog Signalling Apparatus but not, as on the GWR a few years later, automatic train control. Before the system could be extended in use the problem of broken trip-levers had to be solved. Eventually a T-shaped arm was adopted. It is interesting to consider the effect of one metal arm being struck by another which might be moving at 60mph or more. The shock of impact can fatigue the metal and aggravate any flaws so that after repeated blows the arm fails. Moreover, the T-arm was struck by every train passing the signal at caution. On the later Underground system it was applied only at stop signals and the trip-arm was only struck by a rare over-run or in emergency stop-and-proceed working and then at low speed.

Any method of cab signalling which is liable to failure is also liable to fall into disrespect and eventually into disuse. It is significant that the first extensive use of an automatic warning and brake-application system in both Britain and France should be based on the ramp and shoe form of contact and not on a trip-arm method. A number of improvements and additions were made to the NER equipment; including the addition of ramps and electrical contacts, so that there was both a mechanical and electrical contact between track and train. In its most elaborate form the Fog Signalling Apparatus gave the driver the following information:

—When a distant or home signal was imminent;
—whether the signal was 'on' or 'off';
—which of a number of diverging routes was set;

—the signalman's permission for a train to draw-ahead past
a stop signal;

—distinguishing bells for home and distant signals.

The NER system was a determined attempt to improve safety
in poor visibility conditions. Although it was complicated, and
therefore prone to failure, it was a step in the right direction, a
step which apart from the GWR, GCR and London underground lines other railways should also have taken.

In 1921 the NER planned faster train services with the Fog
Signalling Apparatus as a key component at over 2000 signals.
However, plans had to be shelved because of the pending grouping which would merge the NER with the Great Northern,
Great Central, Great Eastern, North British and Great North
of Scotland railways. The new London & North Eastern Railway did not adopt the NER cab signalling system and after a
period of indecision the equipment was dismantled in 1932,
20 years before the Harrow disaster and all the comments which
that accident generated about cab signalling, automatic warning systems and safety in general. A contributory factor in the
decision to abandon the NER Fog Warning Apparatus was the
significant improvement made to the signals on the main line
north of York which was, in my view, a weak decision based on
the false premise that the brightest and clearest signal will never
be mistaken or missed by a driver.

The Great Central trip apparatus was called the *Reliostop*
and was similar to the NER and the London underground
systems in that it used trip levers which engaged a moveable
arm at the side of the track adjacent to and operating with the
signal. This equipment was not perpetuated by the LNER when
it acquired the Great Central, possibly because it had been
applied to only a few signal locations and locomotives.

Within the overall subject of automatic warning systems there
are various types ranging from the elaborate to the simple and
from the advisory to the absolute-stop type. At the elaborate
end of the scale are those systems which give the driver a con-

tinuous indication of the speed at which the train should be operated along with an overriding automatic stop device should the driver fail to respond correctly to the indications of the cab-indicator. At the other end of the scale is the simple train-stop without any form of cab-indicator, as used on a number of urban electric lines, such as London Transport.

The GWR system which was the precursor of the present British Railways AWS, as developed through the Strowger-Hudd system of the 1930s, gave an 'all-clear' or 'warning' audible signal, which corresponded with the indication of the distant signal, and an automatic brake application in the event of an unacknowledged caution warning. As we have seen, the Raven-Baister equipment went a step further because it displayed miniature semaphores, on the cab instrument, which replicated the lineside signals.

In some respects the railways of North America were in advance of the rest of the world with the development of automatic train-stops and cab-signalling. Although the cab-signalling system eventually adopted as a standard by the Pennsylvania came ten years after the NER and GWR systems it was of a far more advanced form because it used an inductive, that is non-mechanical, link between track and train. This inductive link was used to carry information which displayed replicas of the signal aspects on an instrument in front of the driver. On the Pennsylvania the track was divided into sections which corresponded with the signal track-circuit sections. A 100Hz alternating current circulated in each section and was picked up through an inductive link between track and train. This alternating current was coded into pulses of different patterns to indicate the permissible speed for the section: the PRR, like the majority of fully-signalled North American railroads, used speed-indicating signals and not route-indicating signals as in Britain. The various codes appeared in front of the engineer as a row of white lights with vertical representing the least restrictive aspect, horizontal as the stop indication and two

H   121

diagonals, either together or in combination with a horizontal or vertical row, to indicate 'approach' or 'reduce speed'. No automatic train-stops were used with this system of cab-signalling. Each time the indication in the cab changed a whistle sounded and the engineer had to acknowledge the new indication by cancelling the audible warning.

The London underground lines realised early on the dreadful consequences of a collision in the narrow tube tunnels and the train-stop became an essential part of the underground's safety equipment. Its use was not confined to the tunnel sections but was used throughout the system, much of which was eventually 'overground'. A similar method of train protection was adopted for the Mersey Railway Liverpool Central–Birkenhead and the LMS Euston–Watford electric lines. Working in conjunction with the lineside signals, the trip-arm at each location is raised during the time the signal indicates 'stop' and is lowered by compressed air when the signal indicates 'proceed'. With speeds rarely exceeding 40mph and with standard train formations, the train-stops are reliable, as are the electrical controlling circuits. In over sixty years this system has never failed to halt a train which has overrun a signal. The rear-end collision at Charing Cross LT in 1938 could not be prevented by the train-stop because it had cleared in step with the signal which, however, was falsely showing green because the signal circuits had been incorrectly wired during repair work.

At some locations, Baker Street, for example, where the eastbound Circle line and the Metropolitan main line converge, two train-stops in the circuit at the approach to the conflicting junction clear in front of a train only if the driver has reduced speed to a predetermined limit, in other words, there is a delayed clearance because of the almost non-existent over-run. As the speed is reduced each train-stop falls clear and its adjacent signal—and signals are not always provided for each train-stop on time-release circuits—goes to green. This allows trains to come down the gradient from Edgware Road and up to the stop signal protecting the junction while the points are set for a train to or from the Metropolitan main line, which at that point is only just ahead of the signal. If there was only one train-stop protecting the junction it would certainly trip an over-running train and apply its brakes, but a train at speed could go well past the signal into collision with a conflicting train at the junction.

At Moorgate on 28 February 1975 there was no time release or delayed-clearance signal and train-stop at the approach to the platform, at the other end of which was a blind dead-end tunnel. A train came on unchecked and jammed itself into a tangle of wreckage compressed into the inaccessible dead-end. As at Harrow, it was several days before the last of the victims could be got out. Carefully-controlled time releases of approach signals and intermediate train-stops have been installed to ensure that the new BR electric trains that now run into Moorgate can-not run into the platform at more than 10mph, which will pre-vent a repetition of London Transport's worst-ever rail disaster.

Among a number of accidents whose circumstances are similar to those of Harrow was one when an express was derailed at Polesworth on 19 November 1951 because it went through the fast to slow line crossover at 55mph. Fortunately this acci-dent did not kill anyone and only two passengers were slightly hurt. The circumstances of Polesworth classify it as a 'missed or failed to obey the signal' type of accident and it is in the same list as Goswick 1947, Bourne End 1945 and others, as well as Harrow. The findings of the inquiry concluded that the driver of the 22.30 Glasgow–London train failed to observe and act upon the indication of the up fast line distant signal which was showing a single yellow because both the semaphore home signals, up fast and up fast to up slow, were at danger. Although there were no trains in the section ahead the Polesworth signalman was diverting all trains on the up fast line over to the up slow because the colour-light distant signal for the next section to the south on the fast line had failed. Polesworth is a good example of an accident in which a driver had placed too much reliance on the 'expected', instead of always being ready to meet the unexpected. In any hour, in the days of steam, the driver of an express passed a signal about every 30 seconds. The green lights of the distant and stop signals came into view, one after the other and swept by. 'All is well.' 'We are on time.' Unless there is a mechanical failure or an accident to a train on the adjacent track or an impossible-to-avoid boulder or other obstruction suddenly fouling the line it is 'green all the way'.

The Polesworth inquiry concluded that the up fast line distant signal was clearly in the driver's view for at least 6 or 7 seconds; at Harrow the time was about 4 seconds. The questions raised after the Polesworth accident included: 'Would an automatic warning system (AWS) have prevented the accident?' I have used the indefinite article because in 'pre-Harrow' days the Railway Executive and its Regions were undecided about both the method by which signal indications might be conveyed from track to train and by the type of audible warning used in relation to the visual indications. Had the present AWS system been in use at the time of Polesworth, Harrow and similar circumstances, the driver would have received a warning sound on the hooter followed, after a delay of 4 seconds, if it was not acknowledged by an automatic brake application.

The British AWS system does not take control completely away from the driver and there are reasons why this should be so. The automatic warning system, AWS, which is now the standard method of conveying to the drivers of trains both an audible and a visual cab indication of 'proceed' or 'caution', evolved from the Strowger-Hudd equipment which was installed experimentally on the London, Tilbury and Southend line of the LMS in 1937 and officially commissioned in regular use ten years later. As I have outlined, the use of a ramp and a shoe on the locomotive has had a much longer history. All the pre-Hudd systems in Britain, including the extensively used GWR ATC, relied on a mechanical contact, ie a ramp lifting a shoe or a trip-arm striking a lever on the engine. The mechanical problems, as we have seen, especially at 70mph or more, had to be avoided and a non-contact principle was preferable as used in North America for example.

The Hudd inductive AWS was first tried over the 37 miles between Bow and Shoeburyness and 150 locomotives were equipped in 1937; it was selected in 1939 also for the LNER Glasgow–Edinburgh line but postponed by the onset of war. The terrible rear-end collision at Castlecary on this route in 1937 might have been prevented had AWS been in use. The effects of World War II included not only the wearing out of track and rolling stock, without replacements, but imposed a ten-year moratorium on technical development, with AWS as one sufferer.

British Railways AWS has two track magnets placed together longitudinally, approximately 200yd on the approach side of distant signals. The first magnet is a permanent inductor and the second an electro-magnet inductor. The electro-magnet is only energised when the distant signal to which it refers is showing a green proceed indication. A receiver is mounted underneath each locomotive in such a position that it passes directly over the track magnets with a clearance of about five inches. The cab equipment consists of a bell, an air-operated horn and a visual indicator. When a locomotive approaches an AWS track magnet the receiver on the engine passes first over the permanent magnet inductor which trips the receiver. If the distant signal is set at caution, or a colour-light signal at red, yellow or double yellow, the electro-magnet inductor is not energised; after one second the air-horn in the cab sounds. The driver has to acknowledge the warning with a resetting handle, an action which turns the visual indicator to show a yellow and black pattern or spokes. The yellow and black pattern remains in view as a reminder to the driver that he has passed an adverse signal and that he has been warned and has cancelled the warning. With this method of warning, control has not been taken out of the driver's hands and he is free to proceed and to control his train in accordance with his knowledge of the route, the signal location and the braking characteristics of the train. What happens if the driver does not react to the warning? The system starts to apply the brakes automatically after two or three seconds. With a vacuum-braked train, such as the express at Harrow, the brakes would have been fully applied within about 15 seconds of passing the distant signal. If the distant signal is clear the electro-magnetic inductor is energised, resets the receiver and triggers a two-second bell ring. Therefore, a driver hears the reassuring bell each time a clear distant signal is passed.

When the Harrow report was published in 1953 the leading technical journals commented on the findings and on the relationship between the cost of safety and what could be achieved in practice. They pointed out that, from 1912 to 1952, 399 out of a total of 1416 fatalities in railway accidents might have been prevented or mitigated by AWS. At the same time they emphasised that the public must not be led to believe that AWS was a cure-all or that it would prevent more than certain classes of accident. The general technical opinion at the time was that had AWS been installed at the Harrow distant signal it would not have positively prevented the disaster, but it would have reduced the chance of it occurring. It depends on footplate conditions at the time. Had the Perth driver not acknowledged an AWS caution warning, the brakes would have been applied in time to stop the train. If he had acknowledged it, control of the train would still have been entirely in his hands. The *Railway Gazette*, on the question of cost, pointed out that there was the economic as well as the technical aspect to be considered and that in the past some railwaymen had considered that funds at their disposal would be better utilised in applying track-circuiting and colour-light signals on all main lines. A high level of safety on a railway cannot be had by making improvements to some parts and not to others.

7

Laymen and experts: the Press

The press inevitably descended on Harrow & Wealdstone station in great numbers on 8 October 1952. A disaster of this size provided a wealth of material, enough to fill the front pages for at least three days and the inside pages for many more. The individual stories were concerned either with technical factors or with the human interest aspects. A railway accident is always news, not just the great disasters. The odd mishap, derailment and failures of equipment as well as delays to trains from flood, fire and storm are all news. In contrast the frightful toll on the roads is not usually afforded the same coverage in newspapers, perhaps because it is expected, whereas the railway is not expected to have accidents—or at least not frequently.

Reports of incidents and accidents on railways in the lay press often include peculiar descriptions of what happened. Despite justifiable limitations of specialist knowledge on the part of journalists, reports sometimes contain examples of jumbled facts. Many journalists record sensations, the recollections of survivors and railwaymen, but in so doing fail to qualify the specialist jargon used by those they have interviewed. Or, and this is the cause of much misreporting, journalists translate railway language as best they can without checking the accuracy of their reporting. The classic howlers by newspaper reports of railway matters have been with us for many years. For example, the pre-war comment on the first run of a new train: 'The engine failed because of a hot fire-box.' Apart from errors in reporting, there is the attitude adopted by a few journalists which can irritate those being interviewed. Because journalists are, by the nature of their profession, seekers of facts they rarely subscribe to rules of behaviour which will avoid giving offence to those whom they are interviewing. They acknowledge few barriers to story gathering, with the result that they can sometimes tread on sensitive areas. There are instances of reporters invading the privacy of a home or even the wards of a hospital in order to get a first-hand account from those injured in an accident. On occasions, I have criticised such behaviour but at the same time must admit that as we all admire persistence in the execution of a task, then I cannot see why we should denigrate such an attribute when it comes to newspaper reporters. Research did not bring to light any evidence of harassment by the press of the survivors of the Harrow disaster.

In contrast to the human stories, which were extensively reported without too much sensationalism, some of the technical facts were sensationally inaccurate and left this reader, if not others, questioning whether the press had been anywhere near the accident let alone on a train. Naturally, technical facts tend to get lost or distorted in the system by sub-editors. The speed with which facts have to be gathered, processed, written up, edited and printed does not allow a leisurely and careful checking process. At the same time, until more recent times, the standard of technical reporting by the lay press has been low compared with that used for reporting political and social events.

Some of the technical descriptions of trains, movements and equipment relating to Harrow were odd, to say the least. The technicality which caused most confusion among lay reporters and their sub-editors, was the use of 'up' and 'down'. These two words had long been part of the British telegraph and railway vocabulary. These terms had been used before the advent of the steam railway when the Admiralty was kept informed of ship movements by the overland semaphore stations which stood in sight of each other to make a chain of repeating semaphores stretching from Whitehall to Portsmouth; it was always 'down' to Portsmouth and 'up' to London and the Admiralty building in Whitehall. Mail and Stage-coach services also used the term 'up' to London. The railways were among the first users of the electric telegraph, which replaced the visual semaphore chain, and the telegraph meaning of 'up' and 'down' was translated to railway terminology as well. This meant that on the main lines radiating from the capital 'down' meant going away from the terminus – even if this meant geographically going 'up north'. Cross-country lines have been more of a compromise when neither way led to London. So far as the Midland was concerned on its Bristol line, Derby was the centre of the Universe, and thus it was 'up' to Derby. Up and down persist to this day even if, to non-British readers, descriptions, such as 'a down express climbing up Shap' suggest that the author has got in a muddle or this is another quaint old British custom. Some European railways get over the problem by labels 'odd' and 'even', or by numbering tracks.

Among the many reports in the national press that of the *Daily Express*, putting aside sensationalism, echoed the thoughts of all concerned with the implications of the disaster and the urgent need to prevent a recurrence. At the same time when it came to report on technical details this paper, like others, became confused. For example, the Tring–Euston local was described as having 14 coaches. When describing the way in which the up express hit the local the reporter or the sub-editor confused it with the down train because readers were told that: 'The Perth engine mounted the train (local) and smashed down part of the footbridge. It then travelled many yards and fell onto the electric line.' As the photographs show,

City of Glasgow ended up nowhere near the electric line. The locomotives which did fall on to the electric lines were those of the down express, which had glanced off the front of the Perth–London engine buried in the wreckage of the local and displaced to the right and across the down line.

The *Daily Telegraph* was another national paper which I read to get background information. This paper credits the signalman in Harrow No 2 (electric line) box with halting a southbound Bakerloo electric train before it could reach the point where the two engines on the northbound London–Liverpool train, after leaping the platform, would have landed on top of it. It is fairly certain that when the two engines fell on their sides and slid to a stop on the up electric line they broke the rails, and shorted the track-circuits thereby automatically setting the signals to danger and raising the trip-arms of the train-stops. Moreover, the traction supply was cut. Of course, the signalman operated his King levers which overrode the automatic signals but after the double collision and not before or at the time. This is also the conclusion of the Official Report. But the paper's story was far more dramatic, which is the sort of story the readers want—or do they?

The diagram of the tracks and trains printed in the *Daily Telegraph* suggests that the artist used an aerial photograph of the scene as a reference but confused the trailing crossover between the up slow and the Stanmore branch with the double crossover which was to the north of the signalbox. Having made that error it followed that the artist had to put Harrow No 1 box somewhere else. Therefore, it is incorrectly placed between the fast lines and the electric tracks.

Even the local Harrow paper was inaccurate when describing the scenes at the accident. Despite the fact that the men and women concerned came from only a few miles away and therefore the journalists should have been familiar with their work and the colour of their uniforms, the following appeared '. . . included US Army ambulances manned by coloured personnel'.

They should have been correctly reported as coming from the United States Air Force and the paper should have explained what the colour of the medical staff had to do with their generous response. Unimportant, you say. It might be, but if unimportant facts are wrong then what guarantee has the reader that important matters will be correctly reported?

On 9 October 1952 the *Daily Express* tried the religious approach: 'The autumn sun penetrates a jungle of twisted steel, and throws dramatic light on a lone symbol of faith and hope amid disaster. A man of God is on hand to bring spiritual help and consolation to the injured.' This referred to the Reverend John Richards who was summoned to the scene by someone on the telephone saying: 'I think you should come quickly, there has been a terrible crash on the line.' The paper quoted Mr Richards as follows: 'Passengers who were unhurt were tearing at the smashed coaches trying to get the injured out. I found three people in the wreckage. The first was the driver or fireman of one of the engines. He was dead. The second was a soldier. He was dead. The third was a porter amid the debris on the platform. He was dead.'

The leader in the *Daily Express* for 9 October 1952 was headed 'Death on the down line', conveniently ignoring the fact that there was death on at least three lines. It went on: 'In sixty frightening seconds a quiet peaceful suburban platform is transformed into a smoke-filled tomb.' At that time of a morning Harrow was not usually peaceful because there were trains passing through or stopping every few minutes. The reference to the 'smoke-filled tomb' belonged to the more sensational pages rather than the editorial. In the same leader there was a sub-heading 'No foolproof way'. This, despite a few odd words, gets straight to the heart of the matter:

It may be that no signalling system in the world could have prevented the Euston–Manchester (Liverpool) express from crashing into the debris which a split second earlier had scattered across the Harrow line. But is there no system at all which could

make it impossible for an express travelling at speed to can-
nonade into the back of a local train standing on the same line?
Remember Chatham: Remember how eleven months ago
twenty-four little children were killed by a bus in an ill-lit street?
There were strong demands then . . . for that street to be lit up
and the danger removed. But now? There is not a murmur.
And in Chatham the same street is still lit by the same dim lamps.
Is it to be the same again over the Harrow disaster? Will a
committee sit, call evidence, report—and then nothing happen
until disaster strikes again?

Strong stuff? Yes, but very necessary.

A chance conversation with a friend, John Chappell, and a
casual reference to the research I was doing for this book
revealed that he had been summoned by the editor of the *Daily
Telegraph* on the morning of 8 October 1952 to get to Harrow
station as quickly as possible. At first he thought of the Metropolitan line at Harrow because he lived on the 'Met'; eventually
he reached Harrow & Wealdstone station and was confronted
by the appalling scene of destruction which remains vividly in
his memory twenty-five years after, during which time he has
reported on many accidents and great events. His well-trained
reporter's 'nose' led him past the outward effects of an event
into the possible causes. Although having no particular interest
in or knowledge of railways, he decided that one of the things
he had to do was take a close look at the signals which he
realised were responsible for protecting the local train. But first
there were the injured to be cared for and for a time he helped
the rescue teams, particularly the USAF doctors and nurses
whose casualty centre had been set up alongside the wreckage.
As soon as he was able he set off to walk north down the tracks
toward Headstone Lane he was able to verify for himself that
both the inner and outer home signals were at the stop position
—although that in itself was no confirmation of the situation
immediately before the accident.

John Chappell was one journalist who took the trouble to
check a technical detail and to render an accurate description

of the scene and the events. However, as he told me, all stories are very much in the hands of the sub-editors who have the task of moulding a story to emphasise those aspects in which they consider the readers will be most interested, as well as cutting stories to suit the layout of a page. Unfortunately, these well-intentioned activities are sometimes the cause of peculiar and inaccurate reporting.

In the last fifteen years or so there have been improvements in the accuracy with which technical subjects, such as transport disasters, are dealt with by newspapers, in particular by the British Sunday nationals. *The Sunday Times*, to mention just one, commissions experts to write a detailed, searching study of events, causes and effects, along with an attempt to answer the many questions raised. In general, these special articles avoid sensational writing and although they sometimes drag in a red herring I do not think this is necessarily harmful. At least they stimulate thought and, on occasions, have even prevented the suppression of facts which inevitably might embarrass organisations concerned with an accident.

The Moorgate accident on London's Underground railway on 28 February 1975 not only raised a number of questions about AWS and train-stops, it provided a good example of the in-depth technical analysis made by the newspapers. Once again, *The Sunday Times* of 2 March 1975, gave the layman an excellent description of the way in which the different safety devices were intended to operate. In so doing the paper showed the advances made since 1952 with this type of press coverage of a complicated subject.

In 1952 television news reporting was not able to react to a disaster with the speed and to the extent of today's television service. The 'on the scene' coverage by outside-broadcast units was only just emerging from the development stage when the Harrow accident occurred. However, an outside-broadcast unit was able to reach the scene in the evening, having been diverted from Ascot races, and live transmissions were made

from Harrow & Wealdstone station for the evening news programme. The speed with which modern communications and
news services are able to react to events is both an advantage
and a disadvantage. On the one hand people are able to see
events as they happen in all parts of the world, but, at the same
time, all this speed does not necessarily mean accurate reporting. For example, television programmes now conduct their
own instant inquiries into disasters. They can be excellent
sources of information if handled with care, but on too many
occasions the mixture of professional interviewer, technical
expert and layman fails to reconstruct events correctly or
because of misunderstandings the presentation is garbled and
gives a muddy picture of the events which it is trying to
portray.

Often professional interviewers delve into technical matters of
which they have little knowledge so that they cannot bring out
the best responses from expert and from non-expert. The experts
either refuse to be drawn on a particular point or lose their
place in the hurriedly prepared script so that facts are suddenly
introduced out of sequence, a result sometimes of editing
filmed interviews.

A final example of press coverage of the Harrow disaster con-
cerns the number of newspaper comments on why there was no
AWS at Harrow and what was British Railways going to do
about the situation? Because of the newspaper comments it was
decided that the press should be invited to look at the proto-
type BR induction type AWS which was being evaluated.
Reporters at a press conference at King's Cross on 17 October
1952 were shown the AWS cab equipment installed for trials in
a Pacific *Kestrel*. At that time the East Coast main line was
experimentally equipped with AWS track magnets between
Barnet and Huntingdon. Not unexpectedly, many of the
reports published described the equipment as a 'cab-signalling'
system rather than an automatic warning and brake-application
device. Ironically the original BR AWS specification did not

include a visual indicator. *Kestrel*, however, did have an indicator which naturally the press spotted and photographed. How was it possible for BR to tell the reporters and photographers that the indicator should not be there? The indicator, a most valuable feature, was kept in the production units from then on.

8

After Harrow?

What changes have taken place on British Railways since 1952 and what lessons have been learnt from the circumstances of the Harrow double collision? The railways have undergone a number of radical changes in rolling-stock, civil engineering and in control and communication. In 1952, electronics, for example, were not used in railway equipment to any extent, but, in the past two decades, greatly increased use has been made of electronics especially in signalling, in which their small size and weight, cost benefits, and service performance have brought many advantages compared with the electro-mechanical systems they have replaced. Until the advent of electronic units and components for railway use many of the large concentrations of signal controls and instruments, now an essential part of traffic and safety control, would not have been practicable. Large control centres now handle traffic over wide areas and have replaced individual local signal boxes. The role of the district control room has been changed by the use of better communication equipment and, in general, the new centralised signalling and control centres have combined the functions of signalmen and controllers in one operations room, in some cases controlling more than 100 route miles of railway. In normal working with all the safety interlocking equipment functioning and used properly, signalmen in modern power signal centres cannot make mistakes.

During the last two decades the traffic patterns and types have changed from the practices of 1952, particularly on the London Midland Region. Gone are the variety of locomotives and rolling stock and the many different types of trains. Today Inter-city expresses and outer-suburban trains are formed from largely standard coach sets. There are Freightliner container trains and special block loads of bulk commodities, but one looks in vain for the pick-up goods train calling at a dozen or more local stations and yards shunting off a wagon or two here, picking up another there.

To stand on Harrow & Wealdstone station in 1977 is to look on a scene very different from that of 1952. Although the station buildings have changed little, the 25,000-volt catenary, contact wires, supports and insulators now 'roof' over the main line tracks. Perhaps, the most prominent difference is the immediate absence of the network of points and crossovers. The four main tracks pass uninterrupted through the station. The freight yard on the east side and its connections to the main line, together with the Stanmore branch have gone; only the ground-frame cabin, unused and stripped of its equipment, remains to represent one of the interim track arrangements installed in 1964 as part of the resignalling for electrification in 1966, until such facilities were deemed unnecessary a few years ago. The semaphore signals have gone, and now the intense beams of the multiple-lens colour-light signals penetrate night, sunlight and mist throughout the length of the main line.

Immediately after the accident there was criticism of the layout of the tracks and their connections because it meant that up stopping trains which had crossed from the up slow line had to stand on the up fast. This was an inconvenient practice but not necessarily unsafe because there were sufficient signals protecting a train standing in the station; albeit the type of signals and the view the driver might have of them, could be criticised. In 1962 the slow to fast line crossovers to the north of the platforms were moved to the south end of the station so that up

I   137

outer-suburban trains stopping at Harrow and scheduled to use the fast line non-stop to Euston, could use Platform No 6 before crossing over. A new set of crossovers giving the reverse move, ie up fast to slow, was installed ¼ mile north of the station. (Fig 5, page 48.) The track layout as it existed from 1912 to 1952 and up to 1962, reflected the need to limit the length of manual point rodding. To economise on the number of signalboxes the LNWR had, as at other stations, concentrated the crossovers between the slow and fast lines, the branch line connection and the points for the freight yard, at one end of the station, so that all could be watched over by one signalman. Had the LNWR put in a crossover to the south of the station then the old south signalbox which used to control the sidings and the Stanmore branch connections, before their removal in the 1906–12 re-arrangement, might have been retained.

Since 1952 the atmosphere has changed for the better. The Clean Air Act has made a great difference to the atmosphere, so that there are fewer dense fogs, particularly in London suburbs. The horrible smogs, with their clinging, choking, yellow blanket, which brought traffic to a crawl seem to have taken their place in history and Hollywood films. This is a very important difference between Harrow 1952 and Harrow 1977. The air is cleaner, the buildings less drab and it is no longer possible, even if we wanted to, to recreate the atmosphere of the 1950s steam railway.

It was the very steam locomotives themselves which added to the generally smoke-filled air of London and on a misty or foggy morning, as on 8 October 1952, steam and smoke from trains passing Harrow added to the difficulty of seeing signals. Just to the north of the station the main tracks run through a low cutting flanked by buildings and this may have concentrated a patch of denser fog just at the moment when the driver of the Perth express might have received a last minute sight of danger from the outer home signal.

Associated with better visibility in general is the significant change from the driver's position at the rear of a locomotive to one at the extreme front. The view ahead from electric and diesel trains is much better and wider than that available to the driver of a train in 1952. Conditions in general are much better in the cab, yet there are still problems even with modern trains. For example, the panoramic view ahead through the forward window of an electric or diesel locomotive, the steady roar along welded unjointed track, the nearly equal spacing of the signals and the monotonous appearance of the cantenary supports, can induce a state of relaxation and inattention on the part of the driver. The relaxed, comfortable driving position, be it in a train, aircraft, car or ship, while making the driver's life less onerous, has added to the designer's problems. Careful thought now has to be given to the degree of comfort and to ventilation and heating so as not to make things too relaxing. As the same time, 'attention-getter' devices have to be fitted which will prevent a driver either falling asleep or letting his thoughts wander to an extent that he is mentally far away from his train. This aspect of cab design was highlighted in 1964 by the then chief inspecting officer of railways, Brigadier C. A. Langley, who reported: 'One of the driver's greatest enemies today in the comfort of the diesel or electric cab is drowsiness.'

An 'attention-getter' is essential if the driver is to be the final arbiter and manager of a train's progress. If the control system is of a type which if left unattended or unadjusted to changed circumstances, does not respond to signal indications, or fails to observe potentially dangerous situations, then the driver must be given an 'attention-getter'. If the driver is to be only a 'door-closer', as on some automatically operated lines, (eg London Transport's Victoria Line) then the safety of each train is vested completely in the signalling system and the control of the train becomes an integral part of that system. However, if the driver is to be the primary controller of the train so that it is the driver's decision on how fast, how slow, when to accelerate, when and where to stop, then an automatic system must still be provided, so that at all times the driver's actions, or lack of action, are safe ones. One method of ensuring that a driver does not fall asleep or enter into a state of 'unawareness' is the deadman's handle or treadle and similar vigilance devices. But, as has been pointed out by those concerned with safety, too much reliance is sometimes placed on this sort of system. Like other security and monitoring devices, drivers find ways of tampering with them. For example, it was found on investigating an accident that some drivers of diesel locomotives were cutting-out the deadman control—or driver's safety device as it is now known—when the train was going downhill by putting the controller into the 'engine-run only' position so that they could leave the cab and go back to the lavatory.

Above all, the safety and efficiency of train movements depends very much on the continuity of the information link between track and train. The vast resignalling schemes of the last twenty years have brought multiple-aspect colour-light signalling (MAS) throughout many trunk routes to an extent that MAS is now installed over nearly half BR's route mileage. All of the electrified Euston–Glasgow main line is equipped with four-aspect signals, spaced more-or-less evenly every 1200yd or so. The indications at each signal tell the driver the state of the line over the next three signal sections; if he sees a green aspect he knows the line is clear for at least three sections ahead, but if he sees a double-yellow aspect the line is clear for only two sections and he must prepare to slow down ready to stop at the second signal ahead. A single yellow aspect tells him to expect the next signal at danger. Meanwhile traffic conditions ahead might have changed and it is possible that the signal ahead will clear to a less restrictive aspect before he reaches it. All along the line the driver is being fed visually with information which is constantly being updated. It still depends though on his correct visual interpretation of the signal and on his correct action. In other words he must see the signal correctly, he must know what it means and then he must act accordingly. Despite the powerful lights of colour-light signals drivers have been known to miss or misread them, even in expectation to see in a signal a colour different from the one actually displayed, for example seeing in the mind's eye a red aspect as yellow or even green.

Multiple-aspect signalling, although much more consistent than all-semaphore or a mixture of colour-light distants and semaphore stop signals, is nevertheless not foolproof against driver error or misjudgment in braking approaching a signal at danger. It is not proof against a driver misreading signals by taking the aspect of a signal for an adjoining line in multi-track areas for his own, especially where curves make sighting more difficult. Thus an attention-getter is still needed in MAS areas, and simple standard AWS is installed on many routes equipped with multiple-aspect signals. The one disadvantage of standard AWS on such lines is that it can only give two indications, caution and clear. Thus with a signal at red, yellow or double yellow, the AWS will give the same horn warning and the driver has to carry out the same cancelling operation by pressing a button. The visual indicator in the cab shows the same black and yellow spoked display for all three aspects, denoting that the driver has cancelled an AWS warning. Only if a multiple-aspect signal is at green does a driver receive the bell, clear, indication on the AWS. Thus in heavily-trafficked areas with signals closely spaced, drivers may often be running closely behind a train ahead with frequent single or double-yellow aspects. With standard AWS he would need to cancel warnings at every signal, which while getting his attention to the fact that he had passed a caution signal could, and probably would, lead him into a state of cancelling warnings subconsciously. There is then the possibility of a driver cancelling an AWS warning for a red signal ahead, not fully appraising its urgent stop indication, running past it and hazarding the train. Unthinking cancellation of standard AWS has been a factor in a number of accidents in which stop signals have been over-run, so that AWS in itself is not foolproof.

In an endeavour to overcome this situation, particularly on the Southern Region where there have been technical problems in applying standard AWS because of the magnetic effects of the dc third rail traction supply, a new form of AWS has been developed, known as signal repeating AWS—SRAWS—which gives the exact indication of multiple-aspect signals on the driver's control desk display. A standard AWS permanent magnet is sited about 200 metres before the signal to which it applies. From the magnet for about 250 metres to a point just beyond the signal is a wire induction loop carrying high frequency codes which are picked up by receivers on the train. Different codes are used for the various signal aspects. As a train approaches, the permanent magnet triggers the equipment. The high frequency codes show on the driver's display the aspect of the signal ahead which except for green, the driver has to acknowledge by pressing an individual button for that aspect. If he fails to press the acknowledgement button in a given time, or presses the wrong one an automatic brake application is made. Moreover, if he is approaching a red signal and correctly presses the red aspect button but then fails to stop at the signal, an automatic irrevocable brake application is made as soon as the train runs by the signal and off the inductive loops. The aspect of the signal just passed remains on the driver's display as a reminder until the next magnet is reached.

Thus SRAWS overcomes many of the repetitive cancellation problems of simple AWS and, moreover, has an inbuilt overriding safety feature in providing an absolute stop at a red signal. Despite successful trials on the Southern Region the the cost of installation is high and cannot at present be justified taking into account the overall safety record. Yet although simple AWS, modified to overcome the stray effects of the traction supply, is installed on some principle SR routes most of the region remains unprotected by any form of AWS.

Indeed, even twenty-five years after Harrow, only one-third of BR mileage is equipped with AWS. It is true that most principal Inter-city routes are equipped and certainly those carrying trains at 100 or 125mph, but large areas of BR are still unprotected—even accepting that some lines only carry light traffic or are freight only routes. At the end of 1975 just over 4000 route miles of BR had AWS out of the total 11,258. The first Great Western experiments in ATC took place in the early years of the present century. At the present rate of installation on BR it will be about the turn of the next century before it is complete, fifty years after the BR programme was started immediately after the Harrow accident and a hundred years after the first pioneer trials in automatic train control.

Standard AWS has also been extended to provide an 'attention-getter' warning at certain speed restrictions, particularly at braking distance from permanent speed restrictions of two-thirds of line speed or less on 75mph and over lines; following the Nuneaton derailment in 1975 AWS will also give assistance in warnings of temporary speed restrictions for repairs and engineering works. This use requires a portable magnet placed at the approach to the advanced warning board of the speed limit. At Nuneaton the advanced warning board lights were out at night and the driver did not see the board.

There are now a number of continuous track to train link systems in use or being developed which, unlike BR AWS provide two-way communication for the driver. The technology for this has been available for some years now and eventually British Railways might have to abandon the present standard AWS with its intermittent link between track and train because it may not prove suitable for speeds above 125mph. Essentially next generation AWS or cab signalling which could be a continuous form of SRAWS, which has already been on trial, will be used to convey information to a train about speed restrictions, signal indications, and, most importantly, target speed indications by which a central or train-borne computer keeps each train running at its optimum speed in relation to the schedule and to other trains. It can be advisory with the driver acknow-ledging any change in indication but free to control train speed, or it can be supervisory, continuously monitoring the driver's action so that if the target speed at a given location is exceeded by actual speed, the equipment will take over and bring it down to target level. An intermittent form of communi-cation can be provided by transponders, passive packs of electronic equipment situated between the rails, normally dead and requiring no power supply. As a train passes, a signal is transmitted from the train to the transponder which energises it to give a coded reply with details of its location which could consist of its position (for example distance from its starting-point) and speed limit information at that point. The informa-tion transmitted would be displayed in the driver's cab. Transponders cannot be used for normal signalling since the information they give is fixed for the location. Transponders are being installed between London and Glasgow for trials of the 125–50mph Advanced Passenger Train, which will other-wise rely on standard AWS and visual sighting of signals by the driver, at least at first.

In the twenty-five years since Harrow we have gained a better understanding of the way in which people react to events, such as the way in which a driver observes signals. In 1952 far less was known about the ways in which drivers observed and responded to signals and warning devices. With train speeds doubled since 1952 it is now of even greater im-portance to understand as much as possible about human behaviour when driving a train, and about the best form of attention-getter or vigilance device. At five-minute intervals in the peak hours, electric trains race through Harrow at close on 100mph in order to keep to their 80mph average between stops. In steam days it took 1hr 20min of hard work by engine and crew to cover the 82 miles between Euston and Rugby. Today Rugby is less than an hour from London. In the up direction the LM electric trains are still moving at close on 100mph well south of Watford, and they hold their high speed as far as the junctions and curves at Willesden.

Operating trains at 100mph and more needs good signal protection. Without AWS, the LMR, or any other region, would not be allowed to operate at these speeds. High Speed Trains (HST) now known at Inter-city 125 units are now in regular use and electric Advanced Passenger Trains (APT) are about to start regular trial service between Euston and Glasgow. The former give 'electric' speeds on non-electrified track and the latter raises the *average* speeds on electric lines to around 100mph. These two types of train have specially designed control positions in which all instruments and controls are within sight and reach of the driver, along with a clear view for the driver of the track ahead. The cab is comfortable, heated and air conditioned. Yet, as I have already mentioned, in the days when the driver clung to the footplate as his locomotive swayed and pounded along, as steam and smoke obscured his view ahead, as rain and wind assailed him and as his legs were seared by the heat from the open firedoor, the driver was far less likely to relax his attention.

Fortunately, those charged with the safe conduct of trains do not deliberately, except on the most rare occasions, relax their attention or abandon their posts. When they do, safety is at risk. But at the same time we have to recognise that they are, after all, only human and whatever tasks they are set, from driving an APT to operating a signalbox they will, now and then, have an off-day or just a momentary lack of attention. This is why it is so important to provide some form of automatic watchdog which will at all times remind them of their duties. Against the background of modern railway traction equipment there are different monitoring devices available to the designer and which can be installed as an integral part of a locomotive's control system. But in the days of the steam locomotive things were very different because controls and instruments were crude compared with our present standards.

What else has been done to improve the safety of Britain's railways since 1952? Perhaps one of the more important steps taken is the abandonment of the vacuum brake in favour of the compressed-air brake as the standard system for fast trains. With the operation of trains at roughly twice the speeds of the 1950s it is essential to use a quick acting and powerful brake. For the Advanced Passenger Train the initial braking effort at the upper end of the speed range is made by a hydro-mechanical system of turbines on each axle of the train with the turbine fluid recirculating to and from heat exchangers. With electric locomotives, initial braking effort can be through regenerative braking whereby the traction motors act as generators and feed power back into the contact wire.

The Harrow inquiry report mentioned the use of automatic centre-couplers as a method of reducing the effects of an accident by preventing coaches telescoping. Since 1952 all new passenger stock for locomotive-hauled trains and for some multiple-unit sets has been fitted with automatic couplers of the Buckeye type. The modern railway is better equipped to avoid accidents from trains colliding or being derailed and should there be an accident then the stronger coach construction and better couplings will do much to prevent coaches telescoping or collapsing. On the other hand, these safety features do not necessarily extend their protection to the side-swipe accident in which an innocent train is hit by one derailed from an adjacent track. Neither will they prevent a heavy truck straddling the track of a level crossing, as at Hixon in 1968, nor the unfortunately increasing number of mindless vandals placing obstructions on the track.

There are now virtually no wooden-bodied passenger coaches left on BR nor any with wooden bodies with steel outer panels, which in an accident were no stronger. Coaches are now all-metal and for the last decade have been of integral construction in which there is no heavy underframe, but the body

146

itself is a self-supporting rigid box structure, highly resistant to end forces in an accident. Latest coaches, particularly for the APT and Inter-city 125 trains make use of lightweight metals to give strength with minimum weight. The rare accidents of recent years have shown how well the all-steel coach structures have withstood derailments and collisions. At Nuneaton where a sleeping-car train piled up against the platforms and buildings in a high-speed derailment on a speed-restricted section of line, only four passengers were killed despite the fact that coaches were spreadeagled right across the station. At West Ealing where a locomotive was derailed at 70mph on points that changed beneath it on being struck by part of the locomotive hanging down, the coaches zig-zagged over four tracks. Ten passengers were killed when coach ends were damaged but, again, basically the coaches held their shape. The Southern Region, although having had a large amount of new stock over the last twenty years, still has a considerable amount of older suburban stock, which, while having all-steel bodies, was not constructed to the later standards of end resistance. They have steel under-frames but even in some low-speed collisions can still show the telescoping tendencies of wooden-bodied stock. The Southern has gradually been replacing this stock, much of which was built around the time of the Harrow accident, but it will inevitably have to last for a few more years yet.

In addition to the specific lessons learnt from the Harrow inquiry there are the overall lessons of the objectives and results of official inquiries. In Britain we are justly proud of the impartiality and disinterest of our judges and the officers of the Queen's courts. Throughout the world for over 200 years the practices and precepts of British justice have been used as models by other democratic countries. They have also provided a guide to the conduct of courts of inquiry. Inquiries into railway accidents in the United Kingdom have been governed for over 130 years by standards set by Her Majesty's Inspecting Officers of Railways and their modern successors. Courts of

147

inquiry have had to report to the Minister of Transport, or whichever Minister had railways within his department, on their findings so that the Minister can take action if necessary to prevent a recurrence of the circumstances and causes. This is done by introducing legislation before Parliament which will require owners and operators of vehicles and machinery to modify designs, improve operating practices and take other steps to ensure the safety of the public.

Harrow was no exception and, by the very nature of its extent and the affect it had on the whole country, the official inquiry proceedings were attended with more than usual interest. Following the official inquiry the inspecting officer must submit to the minister a report which will include the causes of the accident; all the circumstances of the accident; observations on the circumstances, the causes and the evidence examined or on any matters arising out of the investigation.

Paragraph 80 of the Harrow Official Report gives the primary conclusion as: '. . . I can only suggest that (the driver) must have relaxed his concentration on the signals for some un-explained reason, which might have been quite trivial, at any rate, during the few seconds for which the distant signal could have been seen from the engine at the speed he was running in a deceptive patch of dense fog.' A satisfactory report? It might be argued that it was incomplete because it did not include a full survey of all the possible reasons for the driver's lack of attention and therefore the primary conclusion should not have been given as an isolated statement. The Official Report might give the impression that the inquiry had set itself certain limits and that one of those limits concerned the actions of the driver of the express. It is as if the inquiry went back along the chain of circumstances until it came to the point at which the driver had to respond to the yellow distant signal light. That he did not respond is obvious. But why stop at this point in the report? Why is there no extensive comment on the ways in which drivers in general respond to signals in similar circumstances?

In 1952 and for at least 10 years after, hundreds of drivers would be confronted with thousands of adverse distant signals as they drove steam locomotives with similar cab equipment and arcs of vision as those of *City of Glasgow*. Should they have been told about all this? Perhaps they were but the evidence for this is not easy to come by.

I am in no safe position from which to judge the findings and the 30 year rule relating to official documents prevents a study being made of all the evidence examined at this point in time. It is very easy to sit back and criticise without responsibility. Therefore, although sticking to the questions raised, I am inclined to the view that the investigators, who were men with long experience of railway safety matters, realised that there was little purpose in following a number of hypothetical constructions of events if they had no firm evidence for them. The Official Report is only the tip of the iceberg of evidence examined, and recommendations based on hypothetical reasoning are not good foundations for Parliamentary legislation. Therefore, for a number of reasons, the Official Report limits its positive statements to two factors: the unexplained failure of the driver to respond to the signal and the need to install AWS without undue delay, but without commenting in detail, which might be of use to others, on operating practices which needed changing and on the equipment and design of locomotive cabs. In retrospect it is easy to comment on deficiencies in the design and equipment of locomotive cabs, but at the time it would have been extremely difficult to introduce drastic changes.

The sum of human knowledge is made up largely of experience and learning. This applies not only to individuals but also to groups of people engaged in great enterprises. Those responsible for the operation of trains and the provision of equipment on the London Midland Region in 1952 formed one such group. Their experience and training were directed primarily towards the safe operation of trains. The equipment used had grown from small beginnings over 100 years or more before by a process of evolution rather than by revolution. They had to make do with what they had been given by their predecessors. There were many different circumstances which led to the consequences of the chain of events which formed on the morning of 8 October 1952. Some were unfavourable deficiencies during the slow process of returning the railway to its pre-war standards and equipping it with modern safety devices. However, although the railway had applied standards of safety as required by the Ministry of Transport, it was handicapped from the start by the unique characteristics of the motive power and the shortcomings of the lineside signals. These were the steam locomotive with its driver and controls located behind the bulk of the machine, and the mixture of semaphore and multiple-lens colour-light signals.

Could Harrow happen again? Certainly at Harrow itself with the altered track layout the same sequence could not occur in the station. Moreover, with MAS and AWS it is as unlikely here as anywhere else. Yet who can say that a driver will not inadvertently cancel an AWS warning and fail to stop at a signal protecting a standing train, and by a quirk of fate and timing that another will not run into the wreckage? At least with full track circuiting, if wreckage from one accident obstructs another line to the extent that it drops across the track, the track circuits should immediately respond automatically and place signals for that line at danger. The chances of a combination of the Harrow circumstances happening again are very much reduced by the AWS factor on lines so equipped. There has to be that one additional failure to make the fatal combination. But on lines not protected by AWS? Again the chances are less but not non-existent. On the Southern, many lines carry dense traffic. Even on lines equipped with AWS many of the trains are not fitted with the receiving equipment. While some routes retain semaphore signalling with its disadvantages much of the Southern has multiple-aspect signalling —indeed the Southern preferred to spend its money on better signalling rather than AWS with older signalling. Yet, on much of the Southern, safe running still depends on the vigilance, skill, and discipline of its drivers in reading, interpreting, and responding to the signals correctly. One day could there be one missed signal for the want of an attention-getter that leads to disaster? Certainly the questions can be posed, is the decision not to proceed with SRAWS an acceptable risk or is the public entitled to the added protection it would bring on the Southern and other densely-worked suburban lines? Is the lack of standard AWS acceptable on other lines where it is still not fitted or should it be fitted to all remaining unequipped passenger lines quickly, regardless of cost? In other words passengers' lives or pounds and pence? Yet looking at the safety record of recent years nobody could claim that railways are inherently unsafe. In the twenty-three years from 1953 to 1975 inclusive, in only seven were more than 10 passengers killed in train accidents, and in each of those one major accident accounted for the bulk of fatalities. In 1954, 1956, and 1966 not a single passenger was killed. Who could have foretold that an underground train would fail to stop at a terminal station in February 1975 and kill 42 passengers when it hit the tunnel end wall at Moorgate? Trains had run safely in and out of that station for seventy years. Now safety equipment has been provided so that at Moorgate at least it cannot happen again. In the circumstances of Harrow, foolproof automation has not, and could not, be provided, except at totally unacceptable cost, so the answer must be yes, a Harrow could happen again, somewhere, but unlikely at Harrow itself. Anywhere, though, the dice would have to be very heavily weighted to provide the same odds on a recurrence. Absolute safety on rail, as on road, in the air or at sea, is not possible, and for all forms of transport, the passenger has come to accept that there is some risk. Millions of years ago the progenitors of man came down from the trees knowing full well the risks they would incur when running about the ground. But they did it all the same.

Appendix I

07.31 TRING–LONDON (Euston)
Engine No 42389 2-6-4T built 1934

Coach type	No	Body construction	Built
Third brake	20823	Steel panels on wood frame	1936
	12005	Steel panels on wood frame	1937
	11780	Steel panels on wood frame	1936
	11550	Steel panels on wood frame	1932
	11129	Wood panels on wood frame	1928
	11254	Wood panels on wood frame	1929
Third brake	21183	Steel panels on wood frame	1952
	15202	Wood panels on wood frame	1921
	14281	Wood panels on wood frame	1916

20.15 PERTH–LONDON (Euston) sleeping-car express
Engine No 46242 4-6-2 *City of Glasgow*, built 1940

Coach type	No	Body construction	Built
Milk van	2931	All timber construction	1940
Brake van	30437	All timber construction	1925
Corridor third	1799	Steel panels on wood frame	1934
Corridor third brake	26896	Steel panels on wood frame	1950
Corridor composite	4469	Steel panels on wood frame	1947
Corridor third	1517	Steel panels on wood frame	1933
Composite sleeper	723	Steel panels on wood frame	1936
Composite sleeper	706	Steel panels on wood frame	1931
Third sleeper	589	Steel panels on wood frame	1933
First sleeper	370	Steel panels on wood frame	1936
Brake van	31086	Steel panels on wood frame	1940

The total weight of the train was 525 tons of which 161 tons was the locomotive
weight.

08.00 LONDON (Euston)–LIVERPOOL (with portion for MANCHESTER)
Pilot engine No 45637 4-6-0 *Windward Isles*, built 1934
Train engine No 46202 4-6-2 *Princess Anne*, built 1935

Coach type	No	Body construction	Built
Corridor third brake	26856	Steel panels on wood frame	1950
Corridor composite	4813	Steel panels on wood frame	1948
Corridor first	1124	Steel panels on wood frame	1950
*Corridor third brake	34108	All-steel, Pullman gangways and automatic couplers	1951
Corridor composite	24683	All-steel	1950
*Corridor third brake	34287	All-steel, Pullman gangways and automatic couplers	1952
Vestibule third	27266	Steel panels on wood frame	1946
Kitchen-car	30049	Steel panels on wood frame	1926
Vestibule first	7465	Steel panels on wood frame	1949
Corridor first	1117	Steel panels on wood frame	1950
*Corridor third brake	34024	All-steel, Pullman gangways and automatic couplers	1951
Brake van	30405	All timber	1926
Brake van	30947	All timber	1926
*Brake van	70148E	All timber, Pullman gangways and automatic couplers	1928
Brake van	31755	All timber	1928

* The three passenger coaches equipped with Pullman gangways and automatic couplers of the Buckeye type had reinforced ends and were of British Railways standard design. However, they were coupled to adjacent coaches using the screw-link and buffers, with the automatic coupler heads swung clear. The brake van equipped with Pullman gangways and automatic couplers represented Eastern Region standard practice for main-line stock.

The total weight of the train was 737 tons of which 293 tons was the weight of the two locomotives.

Appendix II

PRE-GROUPING RAILWAYS WHICH FORMED THE LONDON MIDLAND &
SCOTTISH RAILWAY AND THEIR TYPES OF BRAKES, 1923

Company	Locomotives	Passenger coaches	Freight stock	Type of brake
London & North Western	3336	9550	82,700	vacuum
Midland	3019	6120	123,430	vacuum
Lancashire & Yorkshire	1650	4310	37,385	vacuum
Caledonian	1067	3020	53,325	Westinghouse
Glasgow & South Western	529	1605	20,680	vacuum
Highland	173	780	2830	vacuum
North London	107	730	545	vacuum
London Tilbury & Southend	82	560	1905	Westinghouse
*Cheshire Lines Committee	—	580	4510	vacuum
*Midland & Great Northern Joint	101	225	548	vacuum
*Somerset & Dorset Joint	86	200	230	vacuum
*Manchester & South Junction	—	139	—	vacuum

LMS TOTALS:

Locomotives 8988 vacuum
                1149 Westinghouse
          10,137

Coaches 24,239 vacuum
             3580 Westinghouse
            27,819

†Freight stock 372,858 vacuum
                55,230 Westinghouse
                428,088

* Lines operated jointly by the LMS and by its constituents.
† Listed as vacuum or Westinghouse but only a few wagons were equipped with continuous brakes.
(Reproduced by permission of the *Railway Year Book*)

Appendix III

Name	Railway	Type	Cab equipment and functions
c 1850 Clark's	LNW	Contact	Needle telegraph on train.
1852 Tyer's		Contact	Indicator of signal aspect.
Laffa's	Barry	Contact	Indicator of signal aspect.
Jefcoate's		Contact	Lamps, bells and miniature semaphores.
Phillip's	NS	Contact	Siren and miniature sem.
1876 Hardy's	NE	Contact	Siren
Bonnerville and Smith	SE&C	Contact	Bell and miniature semaphores.
Raven's	NE	Contact	Bells and miniature semaphores.
1906 Western Syndicate	GW	Contact	Siren and bell.
Reliostop	GC	Contact	Siren and brake application.
Brown's 'Trainstop'		Contact	Developed in various forms by Westinghouse and Union Switch and Signal companies for suburban electric railways such as London's Underground, Metropolitan and District, Waterloo & City and for LMS Euston–Watford and Mersey Railway Liverpool Central–Birkenhead. No cab equipment. A full brake application is automatically made on a train passing a stop signal at danger.
Boult's	GN, GC	Inductive	Lamps and miniature semaphores for both route indicating and signal aspects.
Railplane Monorail		Inductive	Signal lamp indications repeated in cab of propeller driven car.
1937 Strowger-Hudd	LMS(LTS)	Inductive	Visual indicator and audible horn warning. Precursor of BR AWS.

155

Bibliography

The following is a selection of the many sources studied, and for further reading on signalling and railway accidents and safety. The following publications inevitably provided much useful reference material: *Railway Gazette*, *Railway Magazine*, *Modern Railways* (and its predecessor *Trains Illustrated*), *Railway World*, *Journal of the Stephenson Locomotive Society*, together with the official accident reports published by Her Majesty's Stationery Office and in particular that of the Double Collision at Harrow & Wealdstone published in 1953, with the findings of the inquiry held into the accident by Lt-Col G. R. S. Wilson, the Ministry of Transport's then Chief Inspecting Officer of Railways.

Anderson, Essery and Jenkinson. *A Portrait of the LMS*, Peco 1971

Barnes, E. G. *The Midland Main Line*, George Allen & Unwin, 1969

Blyth, R. *Danger Ahead*, Newman Neame, 1951

Broadbent, H. R. *An Introduction to Railway Braking*, Chapman & Hall, 1969

Bucknall, Col R. *Our Railway History*, author, 1945

Byles, C. B. 'The First Principles of Railway Signalling', *Railway Gazette*, 1918

Coombs, L. F. E.—'The Driver's Place', *Railway World*, August 1971

eebgment

'Visual Perception and High Speed Trains', *Modern Railways*, December 1972

'Harrow—20 Years On', *Modern Railways*, October 1972

'Steam Locomotive Ergonomics,' *Applied Ergonomics*, 4.1, 1973

'The Driver's View', *Railway World*, January 1974

Davis, D. R. 'Railway Signals Passed at Danger', *Ergonomics*, 9.3, 1966

Doherty, D. *The LMS Duchesses*, Model and Allied Publications, 1973

Dorman, C. C. *The London and North Western Railway*, Priory Press, 1975

Engineering, 'The Cost of Automatic Train Control', 10 July 1953

Engineer, The. 'The Harrow Accident and ATC', 10 July 1953

Ellis, C. H. *The Midland Railway*, Ian Allan Ltd, 1953

Hamilton, J. A. B. *British Railway Accidents of the 20th Century*, G. A. Unwin, 1967

Holt, G. O. 'An Early Railway Accident at Harrow', *Journal of the Railway and Canal Historical Society*, May 1958

Hoole, K. 'Cab Signalling on the NER', *Railway World*, February 1963

Hopkins, V. D. 'Unawareness', *Royal Air Force IAM*, 1965

Kichenside, G. M. and Williams, A. *British Railway Signalling*, Ian Allan, 1975, 3rd ed

May, T.—*The History of Harrow County School for Boys*, Harrow County School, 1975

'Harrow School', M Phil thesis

Nock, O. S.—*Fifty Years of Railway Signalling*, IRSE, 1962

Historic Railway Disasters, Ian Allan, 1966

North Western, Ian Allan, 1968

British Railway Signalling, George Allen & Unwin, 1969

Public Record Office: British Transport Collection relating to LNWR and LMS subjects

Reynolds, Michael. *Locomotive Engine Driving*, Lockwood, 1884

Robertson, Col J. R. H. 'Development and Functions of the Railway Inspectorate'

Rolt, L. T. C. *Red for Danger*, David & Charles, 1971

Schneider and Mase. *Railway Accidents of Great Britain and Europe*, David & Charles, 1968

Shaw, R. B. *Down Brakes*, Macmillan, 1961

Stephenson, B. *LMS Album No 3*, Ian Allan, 1973

Tuplin, Dr W. A. 'Some questions about the Steam Locomotive', Proceedings of the Institution of Locomotive Engineers, 43, 1953

  North Western Steam, George Allen & Unwin, 1963

  Midland Steam, David & Charles, 1973

White, H. P. *London Railway History*, David & Charles, 1971

Wilson, H. R. *The Safety of British Railways*, King & Son, 1909

Acknowledgements

This book could not have been completed without the help and the advice of many people and organisations.

My thanks are due to the staff of the Public Record Office-BTC; the staff of the Civic Centre library Harrow, who provided help and access to the local records of the disaster and to the nineteenth-century surveys and chronicles of the district; Dr J. M. Rolfe, then at the RAF IAM, who commented on and advised on the chapter relating to human factors; Dr N. W. Bertenshaw, Department of Science and Industry, Birmingham, who arranged for photographs to be taken from the driver's position on a coronation class Pacific. I am also highly indebted to Meg and David Boswell for their patient reading of the first draft; G. F. Coles who read and advised on the chapter dealing with the development of Harrow and its railways; David Bednall of the Pinner, Hatch End Local Historical and Archaeological Association; Geoffrey Kichenside, who conceived the idea of the book, and for his constant help and advice; P. W. C. Whitton for his advice on the design of illustrations; to John Chappell and John Marsden for their first hand accounts of the disaster; Mrs Carrie Chapman who typed the manuscript; C. R. L. Coles and J. H. Holmes for help with finding photographs. Finally, my thanks to my family and relatives for their encouragement and help at all times.

Index

vigilance devices, 139–44, 151
view ahead, 7, 27, 79ff, 88, 92, 138,
    145, 150

war experience of rescue services, 37
weather conditions, 11–12

Westinghouse brake, 103–6
WRVS, 33
Williams, S., 32
Wilson, Lt-Col G. R. S., 6, 70
workload, 92
wreckage, 24, 27–38